THE CHAI-LIGHT ZONE

The Chai-Light Zone

Rod Serling, Secular Jew

DAVID DEANGELO, STEVEN GIMBEL,
& STEPHEN STERN

CASCADE *Books* • Eugene, Oregon

THE CHAI-LIGHT ZONE
Rod Serling, Secular Jew

Copyright © 2024 David DeAngelo, Steven Gimbel, and Stephen Stern. All rights reserved. Except for brief quotations in critical publications or reviews, no part of this book may be reproduced in any manner without prior written permission from the publisher. Write: Permissions, Wipf and Stock Publishers, 199 W. 8th Ave., Suite 3, Eugene, OR 97401.

Cascade Books
An Imprint of Wipf and Stock Publishers
199 W. 8th Ave., Suite 3
Eugene, OR 97401

www.wipfandstock.com

PAPERBACK ISBN: 979-8-3852-1193-7
HARDCOVER ISBN: 979-8-3852-1194-4
EBOOK ISBN: 979-8-3852-1195-1

Cataloguing-in-Publication data:

Names: DeAngelo, David [author]. | Gimbel, Steven, 1968– [author]. | Stern, Stephen [author].

Title: The chai-light zone : Rod Serling, secular Jew / David DeAngelo, Steven Gimbel, and Stephen Stern.

Description: Eugene, OR: Cascade Books, 2024 | Includes bibliographical references and index.

Identifiers: ISBN 979-8-3852-1193-7 (paperback) | ISBN 979-8-3852-1194-4 (hardcover) | ISBN 979-8-3852-1195-1 (ebook)

Subjects: LCSH: Serling, Rod, 1924–1975—Criticism and interpretation. | Twilight Zone (Television program : 1959–1964). | Judaism. | Jewish people. | Science fiction & fantasy. | Television personalities—United States. | Authors, American—20th century.

Classification: PS3537.E654 G55 2024 (paperback) | PS3537.E654 (ebook)

VERSION NUMBER 07/01/24

To my mother, who has always supported me in achieving my greatest aspirations, even in this Twilight Zone of a world we live in.
D. D.

To Paul, Heather, Zöe, and Liam
S.G.

For Cheyney Ryan. He helps make the world better.
S.S.

Contents

Introduction: A World That Needed Healing | 1

Chapter 1　　Rod Serling's Jewishness | 8

Chapter 2　　Portrayals of Nazism in *The Twilight Zone*'s
　　　　　　　Early Seasons | 26

Chapter 3　　"The Mighty Casey": Striking Out Nazi Race Theory
　　　　　　　with Jewish Ethics | 40

Chapter 4　　Serling's Moral Inversion of Anti-Semitic Stereotypes | 50

Chapter 5　　The Borscht Belt Meets Orion's Belt: Jewish Comedy
　　　　　　　in *The Twilight Zone* | 68

Chapter 6　　Three Rabbis Named Chaim: Neo-Talmudic
　　　　　　　Television | 80

Chapter 7　　Seeing Is *Not* Believing: *The Twilight Zone*,
　　　　　　　Candid Camera, and *Mission: Impossible* | 98

Bibliography | 123

Index | 129

Introduction

A World That Needed Healing

On October 7, 1959, the Soviet probe Luna 3 showed humanity something it had never seen before: the dark side of the moon. The images were shocking to the American public. Not because of what they showed but because of what they meant. The USSR was winning the space race.[1] Earlier that year, the Cuban revolution brought Communism less than a hundred miles from the shores of the United States as the Cold War against Russia continued to rage. The back half of the moon was not all that seemed dark.

Five days earlier, *The Twilight Zone* premiered on CBS with the episode "Where Is Everybody?," a bizarre tale about a man called Mike Ferris (Earl Holliman) who mysteriously finds that everyone else in the world has vanished. Food was cooking. Radios were playing. Life was otherwise proceeding as if everyone had been there just moments before. Yet they weren't.

No matter where he went, Mike was alone. The alienation drives him insane. As he violently raged, he was awakened to find that it was all a manufactured illusion. Mike was, in fact, an American astronaut in training, sequestered in a small simulator room. Having to live devoid of all community in the loneliness of space was the great challenge he was being taught to bear. Carried out on a stretcher having regained his senses, Mike assures the Air Force generals around him that he'll be able to thrive in the loneliness of space. He looks up at the moon and says with the American go-get-'em attitude, "Don't go away up there. We'll be up there in a little while."

From its first moments on television, *The Twilight Zone* walked along the tightrope with the American psyche, which teetered between the

---

1. Kohonen, *Picturing the Cosmos*, 118.

promise and peril of a technologized future that contained not only the seeds of human flourishing but also the very real potential for its ultimate destruction. Television brought instant images from across the globe and labor-saving devices seemed to be able to provide us with unlimited leisure time. All the while the threat of nuclear annihilation was ever-present and growing. *The Twilight Zone* is an artifact of this peculiar mix of hope and dread that hung thick in the air of the middle of the twentieth century.

The optimism derived from an open future in which science and science fiction excitingly intermingled. If it could be *thought*, we thought, it could be *done*. What the future held in store could only be imagined.

Looking forward was essential because looking backward showed the ghosts of the haunted recent past. This was the same year that Yom HaShoah, the Day of Holocaust Remembrance, was first observed.[2] The reverberations of Nazi atrocities still resounded beside the fresh memory of the American dropping of two atomic bombs on the civilians of two Japanese cities, not to mention the grim days of the Great Depression.

Yet, it was a time of uneasy aspiration. The American Century was dawning. Suburban homes with picket fences and green lawns demonstrated comforts that earlier generations could never even dream of. The American Dream was becoming, for many, a reality.

This was especially true of American Jews. Because so many signed up to fight Hitler, the GI Bill allowed a generational shift, a mass migration away from the crowded tenements and slave wages of the sweatshops. With free college and low-cost mortgages, they became doctors and lawyers with nice new homes in the rapidly growing Levittowns.[3]

Jews were starting to become White, or at least White-ish. Antisemitism had flared before the Second World War with icons like Henry Ford and Charles Lindbergh as its emblems, their status justifying their discriminatory leanings.[4] But by the late 1950s, with the bigotry firmly focused on the plight of Black Americans, the wave of hate directed at Jews had crested. There was still redlining and informal agreements limiting Jewish participation in professional and social opportunities, but the sting of being excluded from country clubs could only be seen as minor by comparison

---

2. Young, "When a Day Remembers," 54.
3. Brodkin, *How Jews became White Folks*, 38.
4. Ribuffo, "Henry Ford and the *International Jew*," 203.

to what other groups were experiencing, especially when Jews could simply start their own.[5]

Jewishness was being transformed in the American mind from being a different race to being a different religion among White people.[6] This reduction of Jewishness to Judaism is a particularly American phenomenon. In Europe, for example, there is a long and continuous history of seeing Jews as a race. The concept of a race has long been a part of Western thought. We see it in the anthropology of Immanuel Kant in the eighteenth century,[7] although it becomes even more prevalent in the nineteenth century as the theory of natural selection of Charles Darwin[8] came to be applied to human society by the likes of Herbert Spencer[9] and Francis Galton.[10]

As Galton's eugenics demonstrates, the concept of race is extremely malleable, almost exclusively employed as a way to take those you want to exclude from full participation in cultural, political, or economic institutions and appear to base that exclusion on something objective. Race is a way to take those you don't like and want to harm and of finding a way that sounds scientific to justify the harm.[11]

In Europe, Jews and Roma long suffered oppression. For that reason, they have both been long considered as racially different from the majority populations they live among. It is the need to justify this persecution that forced the European mind to make Jewishness a racial difference.[12] This is why Nazi race scientists became obsessed with hematology. Aryan vs. Jewish blood was not metaphorical to them. They sought the basis of race in the composition of blood. While they are responsible for advances in hematology (look that closely at blood for long enough, and you are sure to find something you did not know was there), but they never did find the sought-after properties that differentiate the blood of the races as they drew them up.[13]

5. Goren, "A Golden Decade," 297.
6. Goren, "A Golden Decade," 295.
7. Kant, "Determination of the Concept of a Human Race," 143–87.
8. Hawkins, "Social Darwinism," 24.
9. Spencer, *Social Statics*.
10. Galton, *Hereditary Genius*.
11. Gould, *The Mismeasure of Man*.
12. Götz, Chroust, and Pross, *Cleansing the Fatherland*.
13. Proctor, *Racial Hygiene*, 150.

America inherited the European notion of race, at least at first. In 1911, for example, the United States Joint Immigration Commission issued the Dillingham Report, which listed "Hebrew" as one of the two subgroups of the Semitic race, both of which were considered distinct from the thirty-six subgroups of the Aryan race.[14]

But after the Second World War, that changed. In 1964, the government altered the official definitions of race when the Federal Interagency Committee on Education created a new set of racial classifications that only had four categories: American Indian/Alaskan Native, Asian/Pacific Islander, Black, and White. In other words, race was reduced to color: red, yellow, black, and white. Note that this does not include "brown," so those whose heritage is from, say, India, the Middle East, or South America would still be considered White.[15]

Most Jews were now officially White. But they knew what it meant not to be. Many, like Rod Serling, were deeply disturbed by American racism. The murder of Black teenager Emmett Till on the basis of the lie that he had shown affection to a White woman stuck with Serling and he tried repeatedly to dramatize the horrific crime for television, but networks and sponsors worried that it would alienate racist viewers and so turned the script down, even as he stripped the story of many of its details.[16]

The GI Bill that contributed so greatly to Jewish socioeconomic emancipation was not equally offered to all who risked their lives in the fight against fascism. John Rankin, a White Congressman from Mississippi, demanded that even though the benefits of the GI Bill came from the federal government, that they be distributed and administered by the states. This meant that discriminatory biases at the local level could influence who got and who was denied access. In the Jim Crow South, indeed to some degree nationwide, the benefits that were used to move Jews into the middle class were explicitly refused to the Black soldiers who had fought alongside them. This was just one example where Jews benefitted in a fashion made unavailable to Black Americans, leading to a socioeconomic divide between two groups that had previously been at similar places.[17]

---

14. Dillingham, *Dictionary of Races of People*, 73.

15. Hattam, "Ethnicities and the Boundaries of Race," 64.

16. Serling, *As I Knew Him*, 93–97; Engel, *Rod Serling*, 125; Parisi, *Rod Serling*, 132–41.

17. Humes, "How the GI Bill Shunted Blacks into Vocational Training," 92–104.

INTRODUCTION

That cultural unfairness led to further alienation. The Civil Rights Movement challenged the structure of the nation. Church bombings and lynchings were in the news. Marches and boycotts closed bridges and threatened businesses. The tensions between Black and White Americans were running high at the same time that Jews were assimilating. This led to White racists being able to point at Jews—whom they were otherwise not particularly fond of—and argue that they were a model minority. Why couldn't these other groups act like the Jews? Jews were different, but suddenly they were not *that* different, not as different as those other groups. Jews moved from being racially Other to merely religiously Other.[18]

Perhaps the strangest place this shift has instantiated itself is in the academic study of Jewishness itself where secular Jews often find themselves absented from the discussion. The contemporary state of Jewish studies in America has become focused largely on Judaism, the religion, instead of the broader notion of "Jewishness," denoting something larger than a set of theological beliefs and a collection of symbols and rituals connected to the Judaic religion. "Jewishness" refers to an entire civilization, indeed a foundational civilization in the Western world. It is one that possesses an extensive literature; ethical, cultural, and culinary traditions; and includes individuals who self-identified as part of the civilization, but did not adhere to the religion. Not all Jews are religious, yet they are Jews.

Rod Serling is a prominent name among these secular Jews. *The Twilight Zone*, his great contribution to American culture, reflects his secular Jewishness. Serling, looking at the state of the world through the lens of a secular American Jew, thought deeply about what it was to be a human in a time when the mooring of society, everything that held things stable for generations, was no longer in play. The only undeniable truth was that life was now different and was going to continue to become even more so. DuPont promised better living through chemistry, while the Manhattan Project opened up the possibility of the annihilation of life through physics. Advances in medicine and the possibility of space travel were mirrored by seemingly more mundane developments like refrigerators/freezers, air conditioners, and vacuum cleaners that made daily life so much easier. The television was followed closely by the TV dinner, changing what we ate, how we ate, and altering the nightly routine of families every evening. The future seemed rosy, except during the six o'clock news and during the drills in school wherein wooden desks were all that stood between students and a

---

18. Goren, "A Golden Decade," 295.

Soviet atomic weapon. The Nazi menace had been defeated in the name of a moral world order that promised "liberty and justice for all," while many of those who risked their own lives came home to oppression and racist violence.

Rod Serling strode into this social-political maelstrom with a unique combination of confidence and questions. In the post-World War II world, it was no longer clear what it meant to be a human. In the midst of both the Cold War and the fight for civil rights, it was no longer clear what it meant to be an American. But, as we have seen above, in this period of rapid suburbanization and assimilation, it was also no longer clear what it meant to be a Jew in America. Rod Serling asked all three of these questions and probed possible answers in the many episodes he wrote for *The Twilight Zone*.

Most commentators have focused primarily on the first two questions only.[19] But as a secular Jew who fought in World War II, the third question was indeed a real question for Serling. Because he was secular, he could not accept the reduction of Jewishness to mere Judaism. But if to be Jewish was not just to have certain beliefs and ritualistic practices, what was it? Why would he have been a target of the Nazis? What did it mean to be Jewish and why were Jews still hated when they strove so hard to fit in and seemed to be succeeding at it?

This volume is dedicated to looking at this third question and trying to find possible answers that Serling provided in *The Twilight Zone*. There are some episodes where this is explicit, that is, where the Jewish content is close to the surface and easily pointed out and interpreted. But there are other places where we have had to read it into the analysis of the series and particular episodes. Such interpretive analysis is itself a creative act. The idea is that it is possible to read these episodes Judaically and derive interesting insights from the use of that particular lens. Maybe Serling meant for them to be understood in this way, maybe not. There is no doubt that some of the moves in this volume will exceed the intentions of Serling. We do not mean for everything in this book to carry the claim of intentionality. There is no doubt that in places we are being more Jewish than Serling was and perhaps even being more Jewish than Serling would feel comfortable being. While Serling may have been made uncomfortable by it, we are not.

Again, we are not making the historian's move of claiming author's intent. Rather, we are saying that Rod Serling was a secular Jew writing

---

19. See, for example, Serling, *As I Knew Him*; Engel, *Rod Serling*; Parisi, *Rod Serling*.

deeply thoughtful scripts about profoundly philosophical topics. He ought to be read as a secular Jew because to not do so somewhere within the interpretive literature surrounding *The Twilight Zone* would be to impoverish our understanding of who Rod Serling was and what Rod Serling wrote.

We thereby undertake this study of Rod Serling as a secular Jew. We will begin with a biographical sketch that brings out Serling's Jewishness. After that we will turn to episodes of *The Twilight Zone* and see wherein the Jewish content might lay. We will then try to watch the show through a "neo-Talmudic" lens, that is, see what Serling was doing as a secular form of the sort of disputation that is part and parcel of Jewish engagement with difficult questions of how to live well. Finally, we will place *The Twilight Zone* in the context of television of the Cold War era, comparing it to *Candid Camera* and *Mission: Impossible*, other shows that were not only created by Jews, but that also featured the concept of empirical equivalence, that is, you cannot always believe what you see.[20]

Rod Serling was a secular Jew in a difficult time. There is a traditional Jewish aspiration, *tikkun olam*, to heal the world. As a secular Jew, this is what Serling was doing with much of his writing, including what he did for *The Twilight Zone*. But he is complicated as a secular Jew. His secular bearing has led figures like him to be too often overlooked by both Jewish studies scholars (because he is secular) and media studies scholars (who ignore his Jewishness). With this book, we hope to bring new depth of understanding to the artificially flattened Serling, by providing an additional dimension . . . a dimension not of sight or sound, but of mind . . . the mind of Rod Serling, a secular Jew.

---

20. A sentence is an empirical fact if it is true and there is a possible observation that confirms its truth. Take the sentence "It is raining outside." This sentence may or may not be true, but to determine that it is true you could glance out the window and look for raindrops, or you could hold your hand outside of the door and see if it gets wet. Two sentences are empirical equivalents if they share the same set of possible observations that would confirm them, that is, whatever you would see or hear if the first sentence was true is also what you would see or hear if the second sentence is true.

Chapter 1

Rod Serling's Jewishness

Rod Serling was Jewish.[1] Given that he was not a practicing Jew—indeed, he converted to Unitarianism later in life at the behest of his wife[2]—Serling's Jewishness might seem to be little more than the answer to a trivia question. But this is not true. Serling was a secular Jew, and that fact was a central element in his identity. It sent him to war. It reappeared regularly in his writings. To understand Serling requires understanding what role his Jewishness played in making him who he was and allowing him to write what he wrote.

Serling's lifetime overlapped with the period where Jewishness in America radically transformed. From the 1910s to the 1940s, Jews were part of a racial minority, but after World War II they were considered White people with a different religion.[3] This meant that Serling lived, like so many other assimilated Jews, as both an insider and an outsider at a time in American history when Jim Crow laws made being a complete outsider deeply undesirable.[4] He got to both enjoy the privileges of being partly on the inside and suffer the disorienting moral conundrum of what was required from him with this new status. He was not responsible for the wrong, but he was now a partial beneficiary of it.

When a Jew walks into a room, they are taught to ask, "What does this situation require of me?" This was a difficult question for the secular Jew

---

1. Serling, *As I Knew Him*, 30.
2. Engel, *Rod Serling*, 72.
3. Brodkin, *How Jews Became White Folks*.
4. Gartner, "A Midpassage for American Jewry," 262.

in America from the '40s through the '60s, but it was a question that Serling wrestled with privately and publicly.[5] Serling's writings, especially *The Twilight Zone*, undoubtedly one of the most memorable television series of the 1960s, is one, but not the only place where Serling thought hard about it. Some remember the series fondly for providing thrilling science fiction and fantasy tales that ended with a macabre twist. Others laud *The Twilight Zone* for using speculative fiction stories as morality plays to convey messages about social justice and war at a time when such topics were considered controversial for television.[6] Whatever the case may be, *The Twilight Zone* still resonates with audiences today and continues to be watched and discussed among fans and casual viewers alike, in part because of Serling's wrestling with the meaning of his Jewishness and with the moral questions it raised.

Most Serling biographies and books on *The Twilight Zone* make mere mention of Serling's Jewishness, usually when discussing Serling's childhood.[7] However, Serling's Jewish background is often not considered beyond stating the facts of his upbringing. Most scholarly work concerning Serling's career ignore the writer's Jewishness,[8] with few serious academic attempts having been made to truly understand how Serling's Jewish identity influenced or resonated within his teleplays.[9]

Admittedly, Serling was not a writer who centered most of his works on Jewish life, unlike authors such as Sholem Aleichem or Elie Wiesel. Serling wrote on a multitude of topics relating to the human condition, typically hoping to offer commentary that extended to all people, not just Jews. Serling was a man with a variety of interests and concerns extending beyond those specifically related to Jewish life. Thus, to focus on Serling solely in a Jewish context would be to ignore many vital elements of this multifaceted man and thus to understand him only partially.

However, one can err in the opposite direction too. When looking at the events in Serling's early life, his personal philosophy, and his teleplays, certain features of a Jewish identity start to emerge. Yet the Jewish aspects of Serling have all too often been left as footnotes, and they deserve greater attention. To neglect his Jewishness is to give an impoverished picture of

---

5. Feldman, *Spaceships and Politics*.
6. Spencer, "Social Justice."
7. E.g., Serling, *As I Knew Him*; Engel, *Rod Serling*; Parisi, *Rod Serling*.
8. E.g., Feldman *Spaceships and Politics*; Spencer, "Social Justice."
9. Klass, "*The Twilight Zone* as Jewish Science Fiction," is an exception.

his life. To comprehend Serling fully, he must be understood in a Jewish context with attention paid to the ways in which Jewishness was manifested in his life.

As with most Jewish American families during the early twentieth century, the Serling family story begins not in the United States, but in Eastern Europe. Throughout the late nineteenth century and early twentieth century, anti-Semitic sentiments were stirring. Anti-Jewish groups acted on these beliefs through pogroms, vicious attacks on Jewish villages in which buildings were burned to the ground and Jews mercilessly raped and murdered. While pogroms had occurred in Europe throughout the nineteenth century, they became more frequent following the death of Czar Alexander II. False rumors blamed his murder on Jews, which itself is odd since Alexander was actually less anti-Semitic than previous Russian leaders. In the irrational passion that resulted from the assassination, an even more pernicious image of Jews was created, which justified pogroms as a means of expelling Jews from Russia.[10]

With the threat becoming more serious and more certain, many Jews headed westward to the United States in hopes of starting a new life devoid of the famine, religious persecution, and looming threat of death in Eastern Europe.[11] Among the many Russian Jews who followed suit by heading to America was Isaac Serling. Rod's daughter Anne writes, "Not much is known of my grandfather's family except that he was born in Detroit. His father, Isaac, moved there from Russia and married a fifteen-year-old girl, Anna, who was deaf. They moved to Syracuse where Isaac owned a junk business."[12]

By the time they moved to Syracuse, they had two children, one named Samuel.

After high school, Sam discontinued his education and took a job doing secretarial work in Auburn, New York, to support the family. While in Auburn, Sam met Esther Cooper, who was born in Lithuania to a large Orthodox family.[13]

Esther's father, Meyer Cooper, came to America alone, where he peddled scrap metal. The fact that Isaac Serling ran a junk business and Meyer Cooper was a peddler is unsurprising. While in modern times

---

10. Gitelman, *A Century of Ambivalence.*
11. Dwork, "Immigrant Jews on the Lower East Side."
12. Serling, *As I Knew Him*, 21.
13. Serling, *As I Knew Him*, 20.

American Jews are depicted as an upper middle-class community populated by doctors and lawyers, the first generation of Jews lacked the financial or educational assets to attain such desired employment. Instead, these early twentieth-century Jews had to take whatever menial job they could fill, everything from ditch-digging to factory work, many in the garment industry.[14] While far from the most glamorous of professions, these jobs were taken out of desperation to survive in America or bring other family members over from Eastern Europe. In just such a fashion, when Meyer Cooper had found enough financial security from his peddling, he brought the rest of his family to New York and opened up a meat shop that would eventually evolve into a supermarket chain.[15]

Sam Serling and Esther Cooper married in 1915. For their honeymoon, the Serlings went to Panama, where Sam accepted a position as a stenographer for General George Washington Goethals, the chief engineer of the Panama Canal, relishing the opportunity to take on a more intellectually stimulating job.[16] After Esther contracted yellow fever, however, the Serlings decided to return to Syracuse, where Sam managed one of his father-in-law's grocery stores.[17]

Upon returning to the States, Esther discovered that she was pregnant. On March 28, 1918, Esther gave birth to Robert Jerome Serling.[18] Due to the yellow fever, Esther's pregnancy proved difficult and the doctor's predicted she would be unable to have another child. The doctors ended up being incorrect.[19] Six and a half years later, on December 25, 1924, Rodman "Rod" Edward Serling was born.[20]

Two years after Rod's birth, the family relocated to Binghamton, New York, so that Sam could manage another one of Meyer Cooper's meat markets.[21] Rod led an idyllic childhood in Binghamton. Despite the Great Depression impoverishing much of the nation, Binghamton remained largely unaffected, allowing the Serlings to lead a consistent middle-class

---

14. Dwork, "Immigrant Jews on the Lower East Side."
15. Serling, *As I Knew Him*, 24.
16. Engel, *Rod Serling*, 5.
17. Engel, *Rod Serling*, 6.
18. Engel, *Rod Serling*, 7.
19. Serling, *As I Knew Him*, 22.
20. Serling, *As I Knew Him*, 22.
21. Serling, *As I Knew Him*, 23.

lifestyle even through such turbulent times.²² Rod and his brother Bob got along well with each other. Frequently the two boys would go to the movies together, then come home to reenact the stories.

Rod maintained good grades throughout school, while still being involved in a variety of extracurricular activities, such as acting in plays, participating in debate competitions, and editing the school newspaper. He was even voted class president once in high school.²³ Rod Serling had an appetite for attention, and, with his cherubic charm and outgoing personality, managed to be a beloved individual in the spotlight of his community.

Although Rod reflected on his hometown with fondness, Binghamton was not necessarily as perfect as memories would serve. While there were no temple burnings or banning of Jewish literature, the Jews of Binghamton did experience anti-Semitism. Jews were not welcome in certain organizations like the posh Binghamton Club and the children's schools intentionally scheduled exams during the High Holy Days.²⁴ As biographer Joel Engel put it, "A sublayer of subtle, but insidious anti-Semitism affected all Jews in Binghamton's small-city 'perfect harmony,' including the Serlings."²⁵

Even Rod Serling, for all the love and adoration he received, could not fully escape this anti-Semitism. In his junior year of high school, Serling applied to join Theta Sigma, but was not accepted due to his Jewish background. An exclusively Jewish fraternity, Upsilon Lambda Phi, did exist, but even here some members disliked Rod because he pursued non-Jewish girls. Later in life, Rod would cite the fraternity incident as his first experience with the tensions that can arise from religious differences.²⁶

Growing up, Rod did not live in a strict Jewish household. Sam's background as a Reform Jew ultimately resulted in religion being somewhat absented from his sons' lives. The Serlings attended synagogue during Rosh Hashanah and Yom Kippur at the behest of Esther, but never otherwise.²⁷ Neither Rod nor Bob would have a bar mitzvah, but both would attend Sunday school.²⁸ In fact, the family was so lenient that they celebrated Christmas.

22. Serling, *As I Knew Him*, 33.
23. Engel, *Rod Serling*, 24.
24. Sander, *Serling*, 14.
25. Engel, *Rod Serling*, 21.
26. Serling, *As I Knew Him*, 32; Sander, *Serling*, 23.
27. Serling, *As I Knew Him*, 30.
28. Engel, *Rod Serling*, 26.

There was no sense in which the boys were expected to hold particular beliefs. Their father told Rod and Bob one day, "I am not a good Jew, but I think I'm a good person. If you want to be very religious, that's up to you. My own philosophy is, I take people for what they are, not where they go to pray."[29] These words stayed with Serling throughout his life.

While he may have grown up minimally observant, that did not mean that Serling did not internalize a sense of Jewish identity. Indeed, in the early 1940s, surrounded by dire headlines from World War II and the horrifying rise of Nazism, it was difficult for any Jew not to experience a jolt to that part of their identity. It led Serling, like over half a million other young Jewish men, to enlist in the US Army in order to defeat Hitler.[30] Indeed, Serling rushed out to join up the day after his mid-school year graduation, joining the US Army's 11th Airborne Division.[31]

He undertook basic training at Fort Niagara and seeing the swagger of the paratroopers, decided that would be his place as well.[32] This led to his transfer to Camp Toccoa, Georgia where he underwent testing. Although passing all of his tests, Colonel Oren "Hard Rock" Haugen decided to reject Serling on account of his small stature—he stood only 5'4" tall.[33] When informed of his rejection despite passing every physical test, Serling marched into the Colonel's office and confronted him, demanding to be accepted. Impressed by his guts and determination, the Colonel changed his mind, thereby making him a member of the 511th Parachute Regiment of the Eleventh Airborne Division.[34] Serling received not only jump training, but also training in demolition.

He never got his chance to help defeat Hitler, however, as they were shipped off to the Pacific Theater. In April of 1944, Serling's regiment landed in Oro Bay, New Guinea, spending about six months in waiting and training. During this time, Serling switched from demolitions to intelligence

---

29. Serling, *As I Knew Him*, 30.

30. There is a disagreement among biographers about this point. Serling, *As I Knew Him*, and Parisi, *Rod Serling*, both contend that Serling volunteered for military service, while Engel, *Rod Serling*, holds that Serling had been drafted. The documentary evidence in Serling, *As I Knew Him*, however, including notes between Serling and his parents, makes it clear that Rod Serling did, in fact, enlist.

31. Serling, *As I Knew Him*, 34.

32. Engel, *Rod Serling*, 32.

33. Sander, *Serling*, 37.

34. Engel, *Rod Serling*, 33.

gathering.³⁵ Just after Thanksgiving, they were ordered to undertake a month-long trek through the jungles of Leyte to push the Japanese toward the other side of the mountain, where other American soldiers lay in waiting.³⁶

During this time, Serling was writing his brother, who was also in the service, as well as his parents. While it is not a central theme of the discussions, regular Jewish mentions do occur in these letters. Rod, for example, mentions that his Jewish doctor told him that the Jewish captains would conduct Friday services for lack of a Jewish chaplain. Sam tells Rod in one letter that the commander of the Jewish legion had died.³⁷

Serling's closest friend in his platoon was another Jewish soldier, Corporal Melvin Levy, the clown of their group. As they trudged through the jungle, planes would drop rations for the troops. About three weeks into the mission, when Levy saw the planes overhead, he joked to Serling, yelling, "Make them kosher! Make them kosher!" Humor turned to tragedy when one of the boxes hit Levy in the head, crushing his skull, instantly killing him.³⁸ Serling helped dig his grave, bury his friend, and leave a Star of David out of sticks. Later, they would exhume him, so he could be sent home for a proper burial. It was a loss that would haunt Serling for the rest of his life.

In the subsequent months, Serling would see active combat against Japanese troops. At one point, Serling had been ambushed, with an enemy soldier aiming a rifle at his head, but one of his troops shot first, saving Serling's life.³⁹ In another incident, Serling sustained serious shrapnel wounds in his wrist and knee. It was not life-threatening, but did leave him with a persistent limp after the war.⁴⁰ He was awarded the Purple Heart for his war wounds and a Bronze Medal for bravery in combat.⁴¹

At the end of the war, in January 1946, Serling returned home, but what he had experienced changed him. He likely suffered from post-traumatic stress disorder⁴² like so many others who were exposed to the hell

35. Engel, *Rod Serling*, 38.
36. Serling, *As I Knew Him*, 52.
37. Serling, *As I Knew Him*, 42.
38. Engel, *Rod Serling*, 44.
39. Serling, *As I Knew Him*, 53.
40. Engel, *Rod Serling*, 56.
41. Engel, *Rod Serling*, 55.
42. Serling, *As I Knew Him*, 65.

of war. He would henceforth be an advocate for peace, knowing what its opposite meant.

Serling's father passed away at the end of his service abroad[43] and that loss coupled with his war experience left Serling aimless and depressed. He had witnessed the worst of humanity and felt little reason to go on.

His older brother Bob had gone to Antioch College in Ohio. Without any better idea, and able to use the GI Bill to cover tuition, Rod followed him and matriculated there as well.[44]

Instituted during World War II by President Franklin Delano Roosevelt, the GI Bill was meant to address two concerns. The first was to make sure that nothing like the "bonus Army" of unemployed veterans that brought down Herbert Hoover's administration would happen again. Secondly, after the Second World War, major changes were occurring in the American economy. Agriculture and menial factory jobs were being replaced by new technologies that required a more educated workforce. So, the GI Bill of Rights was created to convey to American veterans two primary benefits in addition to free ongoing medical care through the Veterans Administration facilities. One was government-paid college tuition. The other was low-cost mortgages. The first created a robust middle class and the second created suburbia.[45] They combined to give rise to what we now think of as "the American dream," a good professional job that allows one to own a home with a yard where the kids can play.

Because the enemy in the war included Hitler's Germany, young Jewish men signed up to fight in outsized numbers. Over a half a million Jews served in uniform during World War II and as a result, the GI Bill was a primary tool for changing Jewish life. Before the war, the children of the great wave of immigrants from Eastern Europe largely lived in urban tenements, working in factories and sweatshops. But after the war, because of the GI Bill, Jews flooded the nation's universities, many of which previously had strict quotas limiting Jewish matriculation, but now with so much government money available, conveniently allowed the Jewish students in. The Jewish obsession with education, which in the old country meant studying Talmud and Torah with a rabbi, was transformed into studying medicine or law so that the family could rise out of poverty. The urge to fight Hitler

---

43. Serling, *As I Knew Him*, 58.
44. Serling, *As I Knew Him*, 65.
45. Mettler, *Soldiers to Citizens*.

unintentionally changed the complexion of life for American Jews like Rod Serling.[46]

At Antioch, Serling began to study physical education, but switched to literature. He found writing a good outlet to help him process his experiences in the Pacific. He wrote a couple chapters intended to form the basis of a novel detailing his experiences in the military and a prose piece called "Transcript of the Legal Proceedings in the Case of the Universe versus War."[47]

Serling also began managing the college radio station, where he wrote, directed, and acted in numerous pieces, some about war. He interned at professional stations including WMRN in Marion, Ohio, WJEM in Springfield, Ohio, WINR in Binghamton, and WNYC in New York City, holding positions from newsroom assistant to writer to music director.[48]

As a freshman, Serling met Carolyn Kramer, with whom he quickly fell in love. She initially resisted his advances, in part because of his reputation as a lady's man, however, she eventually gave in and the two started dating, going steady, and eventually he proposed and she accepted.[49]

Carolyn was not Jewish but Unitarian, a fact that did not make Rod's mother happy. The reaction to their religious difference, however, was much more antagonistic on Carolyn's side. Her father, who was largely absent in Carolyn's life, told her, "I absolutely forbid you to marry that black-haired little Jew."[50]

Because of the pressure, Carolyn urged Rod to convert to Unitarianism and he agreed. Rod's daughter Anne explains it this way:

> My parents always remained wary of organized religion. They agreed that my sister and I would go to the Unitarian Church Sunday mornings when we were younger. This is acceptable to my dad because the messages taught are intellectually open-minded. It is a liberal religion. Nothing is compulsory, and many of the ideals are similar to Judaism.[51]

---

46. As noted earlier, the benefits of the GI Bill were not distributed evenly and the racism inherent in keeping these benefits from Black veterans played a significant part in the inability of Black families to climb the socioeconomic ladder the way other groups did. See Mettler *Soldiers to Citizens*, 22.

47. Engel, *Rod Serling*, 69.

48. Engel, *Rod Serling*, 74.

49. Serling, *As I Knew Him*, 69.

50. Engel, *Rod Serling*, 72.

51. Serling, *As I Knew Him*, 30–31.

While Carolyn urged Rod to become Unitarian, she herself did so, in the words of Anne Serling, with a particular sense of the religion. "My mother, who was raised Unitarian, likes the free-thinking, the permission to believe what one wants."[52] So, while Serling did convert, converting to Unitarianism does not necessarily entail doctrinal alterations.

Indeed, the secular Serling continued to hold onto certain Jewish elements. Anne recalls:

> Throughout his life, my father holds on to many Jewish values and traditions. For years I see him light Yahrzeit memorial candles at sundown on the anniversaries of his parents' deaths. The candlelight glows in the darkness of the room, flickering when we walk by, burning into the following day. Sometimes he stops and stares for just a moment.[53]

She also recalled her father and uncle often going to the Binghamton Jewish Community Center.[54] So, while Serling may have technically converted, he still remained Jewish in terms of certain meaningful rituals and in the sense of feeling a part of the community. Rod Serling was a fairly standard secular Jew.[55]

Despite their familial misgivings, Rod and Carolyn married. They were both still college students at the time and moved into a trailer used by the college as housing for married students.[56]

As an upperclassman, Serling began to shop around some of his better writing. He submitted his script "To Live a Dream" to the *Dr. Christian Show*, which had a script-writing contest. The teleplay is about a boxer who develops leukemia and continues to fight for his life while helping train a youngster to become a champion. It won second place and a $500 prize.[57] Encouraged, he continued looking for outlets, getting two scripts produced on the CBS Saturday morning radio show *Grand Central Station*.[58]

In 1950, Serling graduated from Antioch and took a job as a staff writer for WLW radio in Cincinnati. He developed a fifteen-minute situation comedy, *Leave It to Kathy*, about two young ladies working at a department

52. Serling, *As I Knew Him*, 31.
53. Serling, *As I Knew Him*, 31.
54. Serling, *As I Knew Him*, 31.
55. Sander, *Serling*, 23.
56. Serling, *As I Knew Him*, 72.
57. Engel, *Rod Serling*, 75.
58. Serling, *As I Knew Him*, 78.

store customer service desk.[59] Serling soon found the job unfulfilling, as he was expected to create very low-brow work that appealed to the common person. As a result, Serling began writing freelance at nights, crafting sophisticated scripts, although much of it was rejected at WLW and elsewhere.[60]

The next year, Serling began selling scripts to Cincinnati television station WKRC-TV, including their self-produced series *The Storm*, on which Serling became the sole author once the series started airing episodes on a weekly basis.[61] By 1952, Serling had sold twenty-one half-hour scripts to the station. These included "No Gods to Serve," which dealt with war, and "As Yet Untitled," which took on racism and was based on a true story. He was developing his morality-based approach to drama.

He soon gained momentum in the freelance world as more and more of his teleplays were being produced for national television. Some of the more prestigious series of the time like *Lux Video Theatre*, *Stars over Hollywood*, and *Kraft Television Theatre* were taking in his scripts. Many of these dealt with war, but unlike the shallow, flag-waving, John Wayne approach that was prevalent at the time, Serling's scripts do not blindly laud the heroic acts during World War II that led the United States to victory. Rather, they were psychological dramas focused on the effects of war on individuals. Through teleplays like "Twenty-Four Men to a Plane" and "The Sergeant," Serling analyzed how war can bring about stress that breaks a man. Such men who may commit acts deemed as cowardly in the eyes of the public do not deserve the derision which they often receive. The immense mental strain brought about by violence and murder will break a man at some point, and each man's limit is determined by his individual circumstance.

Although many of Serling's early teleplays heavily focused on the need to recognize individuals within the grand landscape of war, he wrote about a variety of topics concerning the human condition. In sports dramas such as "Welcome Home," "Lefty," and "The Twilight Rounds," Serling explores athletes who must rediscover a purpose in life once the prime of their career has ended.

Serling's big break came on January 12, 1955, when his teleplay "Patterns," a biting drama about balancing morality and success in the corporate world, aired on *Kraft Television Theatre*. It received rave reviews and would

---

59. Parisi, *Rod Serling*, 24.
60. Serling, *As I Knew Him*, 78.
61. Parisi, *Rod Serling*, 28.

go on to garner Serling his first Emmy. It was so popular that on February 9, a live encore performance was aired, the first encore performance in the history of television.[62] The following year, "Patterns" was adapted into a theatrical film starring Van Heflin and Everett Sloane.

He returned to well-trodden ground with his next script, "The Rack," which examined the psyche of a man dealing with war trauma. It received good reviews, not to the degree of "Patterns," but it became clear that Serling was able to both earn a living and deal with his PTSD through the writing process.[63]

In a preview of things to come, Serling's script "To Wake at Midnight" aired on June 23, 1955. It is the story of a former Nazi who wakes up in England after having been in a coma for a number of years. It would be the first time he dealt explicitly with Nazism in particular and fascism in general as a subject for a national audience, but it was far from the last.[64]

He wrote several more celebrated teleplays. These were receiving such positive reviews from critics and viewing audiences that the networks took notice. CBS signed him to an exclusive deal. Indeed, he was the first network writer to ever receive an exclusive contract.[65]

America in the 1950s was a hotbed of racism and Serling felt the need to use his platform to say something about it. He was especially appalled at the murder of teenager Emmett Till and wrote a script to dramatize the horrific event.[66] The network and advertisers were concerned about alienating racist viewers, especially in the South. Serling decided to rewrite the story with the person facing persecution as a poor Jewish pawnbroker instead of a Black teenager visiting relatives. When this was also determined problematic, the character was changed to an "unidentifiable foreigner" and the murderer was to be portrayed as a "decent kid gone momentarily wrong." The town in which the story takes place was also no longer in the South, but distinctly in New England. "Noon on Doomsday" aired on April 25, 1956.[67]

Six months later, Serling's teleplay "Requiem for a Heavyweight" appeared on the prestigious hour-and-a-half-long drama series *Playhouse 90*.[68]

62. Serling, *As I Knew Him*, 82–84.
63. Engel, *Rod Serling*, 113–15.
64. Engel, *Rod Serling*, 117.
65. Engel, *Rod Serling*, 162.
66. Serling, *As I Knew Him*, 94.
67. Serling, *As I Knew Him*, 96.
68. Serling, *As I Knew Him*, 85.

It starred Jewish vaudeville comedian Ed Wynn, whom many had long considered washed up as a performer, in the serious role of the cut man of a fighter who could die if he takes to the ring again, but whose manager owes bookies money so that he may be killed if the boxer does not fight. It received tremendous critical response and won Serling not only another Emmy, but the first ever George Foster Peabody Award to be given to a television writer.[69]

His storied career continued, with more scripts filmed and more awards collected. Serling's notoriety as a teleplay author grew as he continued to write well-received scripts for *Playhouse 90*. Teleplays such as "The Velvet Alley," a semi-autobiographical piece about a struggling television writer who suddenly finds great success, and "The Rank and File," about a lowly worker's rise to labor union president and his fall when he begins doing business with a gangster, were met with critical praise. "The Comedian," which starred Mickey Rooney as an ill-tempered comedian putting on the first ninety-minute made-for-television comedy special, earned Serling his third Emmy.[70]

Perhaps his most important piece for *Playhouse 90* was the series finale "In the Presence of Mine Enemies," which is set in the Warsaw Ghetto during the Holocaust and focuses on a rabbi who urges for peace and understanding of all people and the rabbi's son who escaped from a Nazi labor camp and demands violent resistance. The rabbi's daughter is captured by a Nazi sergeant and then raped by a Nazi captain, whom the son murders in revenge. When the captain's killer is sought, a non-Jewish friend falsely confesses in order to save his Jewish neighbors, whom he has been surreptitiously aiding. When a Nazi sergeant professes his love for the daughter and offers to help her escape, the rabbi must decide whether to forgive the Nazi to save his daughter.[71]

Despite finding great success in his career, Serling was not satisfied. He believed he could transform "the idiot box" into an intellectual storytelling medium that brought engaging tales tinged with social and political commentary to millions of homes every night. The sponsors disagreed. Sponsors did not want their companies' names associated with stories that were depressing or expressed a controversial opinion for fear of losing the trust of customers. As a result, sponsors would censor heavily, especially

69. Engel, *Rod Serling*, 154.
70. Parisi, *Rod Serling*, 161.
71. Serling, *As I Knew Him*, 98–99.

the teleplays of Serling, who was not afraid to express disdain for hateful racism and bigotry. In retaliation, Serling often spoke out against the limitations sponsors placed, which limited television's ability to evolve into a distinguished art form. This earned him the nickname of the "Television's Angry Young Man."

Realizing that he could never so plainly express his liberal beliefs through drama, Serling came up with a clever idea: mask the commentary with science fiction and fantasy. In the late 1950s, science fiction and fantasy were largely understood as genres for children, with such stories relegated to comic books and Saturday matinees. Serling, on the other hand, who spent many of his insomnia-ridden nights consuming EC comics and the works of Ray Bradbury and H. P. Lovecraft, understood the great capabilities of using highly fictionalized worlds and scenarios to address very human issues. Serling realized that censors would never belabor over such fantastical tales, which would give Serling the opportunity to hide his messages right under the surface of stories about robots and humans with magic powers. This revelation resulted in Serling proposing a weekly anthology series to CBS, in which the episodes would only be connected by being stories of imaginary fiction. Serling called the series *The Twilight Zone*.

When Serling proposed the show, CBS was wary. After all, fantasy stories were too low-brow for prime time and the anthology format was largely dead by the late 1950s. Westerns and family sitcoms could be used by sponsors to endorse products with recognizable characters and had proven to be extremely profitable for the networks. Nevertheless, CBS asked Serling to write a pilot script for consideration.

Serling wrote a variety of pilot scripts for *The Twilight Zone*, including an unproduced one called "The Happy Place," an allegorical tale for the Holocaust in which citizens who reached the age of sixty were euthanized.[72] The most important of these scripts was titled "The Time Element," which was about a man who has a recurring dream of waking up in Hawaii on December 7, 1941, and continually fails to stop the attack on Pearl Harbor. CBS paid Serling for the effort, but quickly filed the script away with little consideration.

However, "The Time Element" was rescued by executive producer Bert Granet, who was searching for dramas to air on the *Westinghouse Desilu Playhouse*. While the network did not like the idea of airing such a fantastical piece, both Granet and show creator Desi Arnaz enjoyed the show. As a

---

72. Engel, *Rod Serling*, 180.

result, "The Time Element" did air, but with the caveat that Granet would never choose another science fiction piece for the series again. Despite the anticipated poor reception, "The Time Element" was received well critically and garnered the series the most fan letters for a particular episode that year.[73] Naturally, the overwhelmingly positive reception prompted CBS to bring *The Twilight Zone* to life.

On October 2, 1959, at 10:00 PM, America was introduced to the fifth dimension beyond sight and sound with the episode "Where Is Everybody?" *The Twilight Zone* ran for five seasons, from 1959 to 1964 on CBS. Serling wrote ninety-two of the 156 episodes and was the show's executive producer. He, of course, is best remembered for having appeared in the program during the opening theme, for an introductory comment, and for a closing comment. The show was notable for its inability to be pigeonholed in a genre. Some episodes were science fiction, others fantasy, historical drama appeared, as did horror, and yet others were comedies. Viewers would tune in, unsure what it was they were going to see, yet tune in they did. There was always a strong moral sense written into the scripts. The series won a Golden Globe for Serling as producer and two Emmys for Serling's writing.

After the run of *The Twilight Zone*, Serling continued to write. In 1965, he created a short-lived Western, *The Loner*, which sought to take the then-popular format and elevate the content, to make the characters more human, and to reduce the senseless violence and implicit racism.[74] The series follows a Union cavalry captain named William Colton (Lloyd Bridges) who travels out West to redefine himself after the Civil War ends. The stories centered on Colton meeting people and aiding them in resolving personal issues. As per usual with Serling, the episodes were used to express Serling's opinion on a number of topical issues, such as racism against Native Americans, gun violence, and PTSD as a result of war. Neither the network nor the audience expressed great interest in *The Loner*, resulting in the series being cancelled after a single, twenty-six-episode season.

When *The Loner* ended in 1966, Serling found himself for the first time in seven years not working on a weekly series of his own creation. While determining his next big project and not having as many offers pouring in as during the mid-1950s, Serling began taking small acting jobs in which he served as a spokesperson in numerous commercials and made

---

73. Parisi, *Rod Serling*, 185–88.
74. Sander, *Serling*, 205–6.

appearances on game shows. He also provided voice narration for the documentary series *The Undersea World of Jacques Cousteau*.[75]

Although in the late 1960s Serling took jobs that gave into the commercialism that he fought so hard against during the early 1950s, he still managed to contribute some notable works between 1966 and 1970. Serling wrote one of the first TV movies, called *The Doomsday Flight*, which generally received positive critical reviews. He also scripted the initial draft for the 1968 classic science fiction movie *Planet of the Apes*. Although screenwriter Michael Wilson rewrote much of the script, the film did maintain the basic premise and the iconic twist ending that Serling devised, which was enough to earn him a screen credit.[76] On February 2, 1970, Serling's "Storm in Summer," a story about a Jewish deli owner forming a bond with an inner-city Black child, aired on the anthology series *Hallmark Hall of Fame*. Serling's return to the anthology format won him his sixth and final Emmy.[77]

Of all the work Serling did for television after *The Twilight Zone*, his most famous creation would likely be the television series *Night Gallery*. In 1963, Serling wrote a short-story collection titled *Rod Serling's Triple W: Witches, Warlocks, and Werewolves*. After *The Twilight Zone*'s cancellation, Serling began talking with networks to adapt his collection into an anthology made-for-TV movie. In 1969, NBC made a deal with Serling to develop an anthology film titled *Night Gallery*, in which two of the three vignettes would be adaptations of Serling's short stories. The series served as the pilot for a television series of the same name.

NBC's *Night Gallery* was a series that resembled *The Twilight Zone* but focused more on tales of horror. The series ran for three seasons, from 1970–73.[78] Unfortunately, the anthology format was where the similarities between *Night Gallery* and *The Twilight Zone* ended. *Night Gallery* never attained the heights of *The Twilight Zone*, in large part because Serling did not have autonomy over the show. NBC's executives gave creative control to executive producer Jack Laird, who largely excluded Serling from decisions such as casting and which stories would be filmed for the series. Laird even edited some of Serling's scripts without his consent.[79]

75. Parisi, *Rod Serling*, 453–55.
76. Parisi, *Rod Serling*, 322.
77. Parisi, *Rod Serling*, 353.
78. Serling, *As I Knew Him*, 190–94.
79. Parisi, *Rod Serling*, 360–62.

While Serling may have been restricted in his involvement with *Night Gallery*, his contributions to the series were significant. Serling acted as the series' on-screen host for all three seasons. He also wrote some of the series most memorable episodes. A first season episode scripted by Serling, "They're Tearing Down Tim Riley's Bar," was nominated for an Emmy.[80] Interestingly, Serling also turned in an explicitly Jewish story with season 2's "The Messiah on Mott Street," which centers on a dying Jewish man who believes that the Messiah is arriving. While not especially deep, episodes like "Lindemann's Catch" and "The Doll" exhibited Serling's strength for writing fun fantasy and horror stories.

After *Night Gallery* went off the air, Serling spent much of his time not in Hollywood but at his lake house in New York. He continued working on television projects, but he also tried his hand at writing one of the great American novels. One of Serling's book drafts, titled *X Number of Days*, concerns a group of American soldiers attempting to bring peace to a post-Holocaust Germany.[81] Serling also lectured at Ithaca College on television and mass media.

For his entire life, Serling was addicted to cigarettes, smoking upward of four or five packs a day. The constant smoking led to Serling developing Berger's disease in his right index finger, which is characterized by an inflammation of blood vessels. Unfortunately, Serling did not comply with doctor's orders to minimize his smoking. This addiction, coupled with insomnia and an intensive work schedule, left Serling in poor health. On June 28, 1975, at the age of fifty, Serling passed away after a heart attack experienced after undergoing bypass surgery.

While Serling may not be well known for his Jewish identity, those closest to Serling honored him in death as a Jew. Serling's close friend Dick Berg made note of Serling's Jewishness in his eulogy:

> Where Rod's peers may have anguished over the creative process, Rod woke up each day saying, "Let me tell you a story." This was his badge, his thrust, his passkey into our lives. He was eternally the new boy on the block trying to join our games. And he penetrated the circle by regaling us with those many fragments of his Jewish imagination.[82]

---

80. Parisi, *Rod Serling*, 396.
81. Engel, *Rod Serling*, 325.
82. Parisi, *Rod Serling*, xiii.

Anne Serling in her memoir recounts frantically searching for Yahrzeit candles to burn on the anniversary of her father's passing.[83] These gestures speak highly of the fact that the people in Serling's personal life wanted to respect Serling in his death as he was born into the world: a member of the tribe.

When we look at the life and writing of Rod Serling, we must account for the context. Much of that is the social-political environment of post–World War II America, wrestling with the existential threat of the Cold War, a changing economy, and Jim Crow racism. But also present was Rod Serling's secular Jewishness. It informed the way he saw the world and the moral stances he adopted toward it. To not understand Serling as the secular Jew he was is to not fully understand Serling. It is to that end that this volume is dedicated.

---

83. Serling, *As I Knew Him*, 300.

Chapter 2

Portrayals of Nazism in *The Twilight Zone*'s Early Seasons

IF ONE WERE TO ask random people on the street to name a Jewish holiday, the most popular answer would be "Hanukkah," which has acquired the status of the Jewish Christmas. While Christmas is one of the two most important holidays on the Christian calendar, Hanukkah is traditionally one of the lesser important Jewish holidays. It is little mentioned in the Talmud, much of the focus on contrasting views about how to light the candles: ought one light a single candle the first night, two candles on the second night, and so on, thereby increasingly honoring the miracle as the holiday passes; or, rather, should one light eight on the first night, seven on the second night, decreasing as the week goes as the oil would have decreased? It is the miracle of a single day's oil lasting for eight days that gets the focus.[1]

But the story of Hanukkah is largely the story of a victory of war, where the smaller, outmanned ragtag army rose up to defeat a much stronger, wealthier, better trained enemy. It is the story of the Maccabees, Jewish tough guys who fought and defeated the legendary Greeks, establishing the Hasmonean dynasty of kings. In most cultures, the story of an underdog military victory like this would be cause for chest pounding and pointing to the victors as evidence of greatness as established through "trial by combat."[2] But it is exactly this element that made the ancient rabbis uneasy, the holiday being completely absented from the Mishna of the Talmud.[3]

1. Zeitlin, "Hanukkah: Its Origin and Its Significance."
2. Rhyder, "Festivals and Violence," 66–70.
3. Steinsaltz, *The Essential Talmud*, 127.

Toughness in battle is not what they thought deserves to be foregrounded and celebrated.

The core of Judaism is not found in taking power over the other, in defeating them and subjugating them. It is not seen in the glory of battle, in individual efforts and feats of strength and bravery, in vanquishing others even for a cause held dear to the community. Rather, the heart of Judaism is to be found in carrying out the mitzvot, in humility before God, in following the Halakhic law, God's commands that are contained in the Torah.

These laws apply equally to everyone. "Equality before the law" is the heart of the Jewish approach to life. No matter who you are, the law applies to you just as much as anyone else. The Talmud contains a large number of passages on how to follow the law in specific circumstances, but it would not matter who found themselves in that lived context, this is how to do the right thing according to God's law.

For this reason, it is not the military victory, but rather the miracle of the oil that is central to the remembrance and observance of Hanukkah. In raiding Solomon's Temple, the Greeks smashed all of the containers of sanctified olive oil, which was needed for the eternal light, a lamp that should always burn in honor of God. Only a single container of oil remained, enough just for one day's burning. It would take eight days to make more. Somehow, that one day's worth of oil lasted all eight days until the stock could be replaced. It is not the military victory that is celebrated but the miracle of getting eight days for the price of one—even the Talmud celebrates paying wholesale.

Where Hanukkah is given short-shrift by the ancient rabbis, we find much more time and discussion dedicated to another holiday. For Christians, the holiest days of the year are the holidays that align with the vernal and winter equinoxes, Easter and Christmas. Religiously for Jews, Passover, the spring holiday, is far more important than Hanukkah, the winter one.

On Passover, Jews are commanded to tell the story of the exodus from Egypt. In telling it, the Haggadah has Jews quote Exodus 13:8 aloud in front of their gathered family. This biblical text speaks of the rescue of the Jews from bondage in Egypt as if the readers themselves were there: "this is because of what God did for *me* when he brought *me* forth out of the land of Egypt."[4] Indeed, there are to be seders on the first two nights. It is not enough to tell the story once, but it should be told twice. It is that central.

---

4. Bronstein, *A Passover Haggadah*, 32.

The point of the story is that it provides evidence for the fundamental aspect of Judaism—the covenant between God and the Jewish people. If the Jews agree to follow the Halakhic law, then God agrees to look out for them in times of trouble. The covenant that Abraham agreed to on behalf of those who would come after him forms the core of Judaism.

The story of the exodus is evidence that God will honor his part of the bargain. The story is repeated because it is crucial to know that the covenant is still in effect and thereby Jews are required to continue to hold up their end of the deal. In the story, God alone is the tough one. God levies the plagues, the Jews run away. They cross the Red Sea, God closes the passageway drowning Pharaoh's army. God could have freed the Jews by arming them and allowing them to inflict the harm, but instead the Jews passively beat a hasty retreat.

There is, of course, one episode in the exodus story in which a Jew chooses violence. Wandering in the dessert, the Jews require water. God tells Moses to speak to a rock and water will come forth. Instead of using words, Moses strikes the rock with his staff. Water did pour out of the rock, but because he chose self-aggrandizing violence over the pacifist use of words of praise for God, Moses was punished. He would lead his people to the promised land of milk and honey, but would not be allowed in himself. A patriarch of the religion, for the crime of being unnecessarily physically violent, would suffer the ultimate penalty, not partaking in the gift God gave the Jews.

But then everything changed in the 1940s. The Jews were abandoned in the work and death camps of Europe. How could one see what happened in the Holocaust and not feel that the covenant had been breached? What sense was there in the old ways, based upon a bargain that seemed to no longer hold? In the shadow of the Shoah, it seemed that Judaism itself had to be re-understood. This became the central Jewish theological project, even for those who were culturally Jewish, but did not believe in God. In light of genocidal hatred that could spring up in the seemingly most cultured of places, how ought one live?

Some of the theistically-oriented decided that nothing should change. Others radically altered Judaism, contending that if God would not be there to defend the Jews, the Jews would have to do it themselves. With the establishment of the modern state of Israel, a brand of Zionist militarism replaced the original Judaism. Others, saw value in the old approach, but struggled with how to make it fit with a modern, science-based worldview.

It is here that we find Rod Serling, culturally Jewish, seeing the democratic ethic of equality before the law as fundamental, yet having to live in a world in which the moral decision was often not made. How, without the protection of an all-being, but maintaining the value of a law-based, interpretive tradition, could one live a good human life? How ought we make sense of the evil around us and how could we keep ourselves from being lured away from the good toward its glorification of violence? These are the questions at the heart of four episodes of *The Twilight Zone*, each broadcast in one of the first four seasons.

The Twilight Zone is unusual in the history of broadcast television in that it is one of the few programs to cut broadly across standard genres. With most shows, viewers tune in with a preexisting understanding of what sort of entertainment they will be provided. *The Twilight Zone* did have a running theme of the supernatural and macabre, but individual episodes might be science fiction, horror, or even comedy. What unified the *Twilight Zone* approach, coming directly from Serling's moral vision for the program, was not part of the form, but rather the content. The standard coherent element is that the episodes should be understood as modern-day morality plays. There was often a black and white ethical message contained at the heart of the story, regardless of how the story was told.

We especially see this sort of black and white moralizing in the series' regular employment of Nazism in its plots. After World War II, the genocidal effects of anti-Semitism became clear and Serling is clearly using his place as central writer of *The Twilight Zone* to make sure that the slogan "Never again" would be the case. In the first four seasons of *The Twilight Zone*, explicit references to Nazism are made once a season with increasing focus and increasing intensity. In this cross-season series of episodes, Serling wanted to make sure that, as nationalism rose during the McCarthy period, we never forgot the dangers of nationalism, White supremacy, and militarism.

JUDGMENT NIGHT

In the first season, Serling wrote the tenth episode "Judgement Night," first broadcast on December 4, 1959, in which a mysterious man named Carl Lanser, portrayed by Nehemiah Persoff, appears on a British passenger ship, the *SS Queen of Glasgow*, sailing peacefully across the Atlantic during World War II. Lanser has a German accent, an intimate knowledge of

U-boat tactics, and a sense of foreboding attached to a specific moment in the near future. He is unable to remember boarding the ship and there is no record of his being a passenger, but he is constantly and obsessively driven to warn everyone on board of a vague coming calamity. As he meets and mingles with the others on the ship, all of whom seem unremarkably normal, he becomes more and more agitated at their impending doom.

His concern, it turns out is warranted. The *SS Queen of Glasgow* is being tracked by a Nazi U-boat with the intent of sinking it, despite knowing that the ship is in no way connected to the war effort, exactly the state of affairs that has Lanser upset.

Just before the moment where the harmless ship is indeed sunk by a Nazi submarine, the focus shifts from the ship being torpedoed to the submarine that launched the torpedo. On the submarine, a junior Nazi officer, Lt. Mueller, played by James Franciscus, voices moral concern over the murder of innocents in a monologue he delivers to his superior officer, who is behind the plot. He speaks eloquently about good and evil and the retribution of those who place themselves on the wrong side of the line. It is a humanizing moment for someone in a German uniform.

But his words fall on deaf ears. The captain, who relished the opportunity to sink the enemy civilian ship, turns out to be Lanser. In a twist on Friedrich Nietzsche's eternal recurrence crossed with the perverse converse of the Golden Rule, Lanser is doomed to become a victim of his own evil decision, reliving the fate of those he killed over and over for all eternity.

The eternal recurrence (*ewige Wiederkunft*) is a notion Nietzsche presents in *The Gay Science* wherein the temporal topology of existence is not linear, but circular.[5] From the classical picture of reality championed by Isaac Newton, "[a]bsolute, true, and mathematical time, of itself, and from its own nature, flows equably without relation to anything external."[6] This flow is linear, leading from the past to the future. But Nietzsche asks why time flows from past to future. Is it not possible that the future wraps back to the past and that instead of a timeline, we have a time loop?

This is the initial episode of the Nazi series and, in a certain sense, the gentlest. It takes a single individual Nazi officer who chooses to knowingly commit a single war crime out of a general sense of hatred. The victims are mostly British, none overtly identifiable as Jewish. As a member of this series of episodes, it simply sets the tone that Nazism was bad, something

---

5. Nietzsche, *The Gay Science*, 273.
6. Newton, *Principia*, 6.

that, especially in the timeframe of *The Twilight Zone*, mere years from the end of the Second World War, would not need much motivation.

THE MAN IN THE BOTTLE

In the second season, Serling wrote the second episode, "The Man in the Bottle," first aired on October 7, 1960, which retells the story from *1001 Tales from the Arabian Nights* of the freeing of the djinni.[7] The protagonists are a good-hearted couple, Arthur (Luther Adler) and Edna Castle (Vivi Janiss), who own a troubled curiosity shop. Purchasing and cleaning an old oil lamp, they free a djinni (Joseph Ruskin), who, in gratitude for his freedom, offers the Castles four wishes. But he warns them to think carefully about the question because unintended consequences often accompany met wishes.

Arthur scoffs at the djinni, disbelieving in the power. When the djinni insists, Arthur asks that a crack in a glass display case be fixed. Amused at the simplicity of the wish, the djinni fixes the glass. This was enough to convince the Castles that the offer is real. They now have three wishes left.

With their second wish, the Castles predictably want wealth, requesting a million dollars. The djinni grants the wish and a pile of cash appears. The first thing the good-hearted Castles do is help all of their neighbors, who were struggling as well. As word spreads of the newfound wealth and generosity of the Castles, the store is overrun with those looking for a handout and the Castles happily oblige. When the crowd subsides, the Castles are left with only a moderate amount of the money, but feel good for having helped their neighbors and are content with the remainder that would allow them to save their struggling business.

However, in through the door strolls the tax collector from the Internal Revenue Service. They must pay the taxes on the entire million dollars and that just happens to come to the amount they have left. After their second wish, the Castles have nothing more than they had when they started. The wish amounted to nothing in the end.

Disillusioned with money, they then move to power. Should Arthur become the president of the United States? No, not enough power because America is a democracy and the power really resides with the people. Arthur decides that instead he should wish to be the absolute ruler of an

---

7. Wiggin and Smith, *The Arabian Nights*, 52–67.

autocracy, a country that possess an absolute ruler whose every demand would be automatically obeyed.

When the djinni grants this wish, Arthur finds himself as Adolf Hitler. But he is not Hitler in the 1930s during the rise of Nazism. Rather, Arthur turns into Hitler at the end of World War II as the Third Reich is losing the war and the Allies are closing in. Arthur has become Hitler just mere moments before he commits suicide. Technically, he did become a ruler with absolute power, but not in a way that Arthur could ever actually exercise the power, only experience the most negative personal consequences of it.

The irony of the move is that Serling is inverting a classic anti-Semitic trope. For centuries, Jews have been vilified as power-hungry manipulators who control the world and create suffering among non-Jews for the benefit of the Jewish minority. Whether it is the Rothschilds who pull the strings of European monarchs or George Soros who does the same with the leaders of Western democracies, the Elders of Zion or Jews in Hollywood who have a secret cabal, or the Illuminati who operate from the shadows, Jews are supposedly the hidden power behind what appears to be the real power. When Arthur, who shows no sense of being Jewish, asks the djinni to be transformed into the caricature put forward by the anti-Semites, he ends up not only not becoming Jewish, but indeed ends up as the ultimate anti-Jew. Serling flips the image used to justify hatred of Jews, showing it to be occupied in real life not by Jews but by the moral monster who sought to eradicate the Jews.

Serling's sense of cosmic justice is served by the fact that Arthur was not only made into an individual of the greatest evil, but placed at a time in Hitler's life where the undesirability of the move failed to fully satisfy the desire. Arthur, by being turned into Hitler as the Germans were on the verge of losing the war and Hitler committing suicide, does get his request literally met—he did become a despot whose every command would be unquestioningly followed—but this comes to be without achieving the feeling of power he craved. The djinni has satisfied the letter of the wish, without satisfying the substance. Not only are the viewers thereby given the image of Hitler as morally undesirable, but also reminded of his ultimate failing. Hitler's power was portrayed as self-destructive.

With just one wish left, Arthur asks to return to his former life. The djinni allows the Castles' life to go back to normal, just as in the book of Job where Satan takes everything from Job, but in the end Job is left with the opportunity to create normal and he does. The Castles have not found any advantage from their wishes because they were self-interested, but at least they had the glass fixed on their display case ... until in the parting shot, a broom gets knocked over, shattering the glass.

DEATH'S HEAD REVISITED

The Nazi references in these first two episodes was restrained—Nazis as war criminals and Hitler as undesirable. In the final two, however, the tone switches and Serling became increasingly explicit in the portrayal of the evil of Nazism and the danger it remained, despite Germany's defeat.

In the ninth episode of the third season, first broadcast on November 10, 1961, Serling's script "Death's Head Revisited" has the character Gunther Lutze (Oscar Beregi Jr.) return to Dachau on holiday after the war in order to remind himself of "the good old days."

Lutze had been a sadistic SS captain at the camp who delighted in the viciousness with which he tortured the Jewish prisoners. It is made clear that Lutze not only enjoyed inflicting pain, but relished the opportunity to devise new and increasingly terrible means of punishment that coupled physical with psychological torment. As he tours the abandoned camp, he thinks fondly of his creative handiwork.

But upon his return, he comes face-to-face with the ghosts of all those he tortured. In this supernatural form, they possess extrasensory abilities. They close the gate, locking Lutze in the camp. The dynamic of control has become inverted. Now, the prisoners have the power and the guard is at their mercy.

The prisoners tell Lutze that they are going to put him on trial for his crimes. Charges are produced and Lutze is given an opportunity to mount a defense. Fairness, decorum, and respect for the rule of law are observed by those to whom it had been denied. On the one hand, this is odd, as the jury is made up of the victims who not only *have* but in a sense *are* evidence for the prosecution. They *know* the truth. They do not need a process to arrive at it. But it is clear that Serling is drawing a distinction between Lutze and his victims. Lutze used his power indiscriminately in order to harm those who were less powerful, whereas the prisoners, who find themselves now in the position of power, instead seek justice through a procedure that grants Lutze dignity. Of course, the procedure is not entirely fair, as the victims make up the jury, clearly not an objective, disinterested group, but it is at least a process with as much fairness as the context would allow, even if not perfect. Despite the fact that they would be perfectly justified in simply seeking vengeance, they instead seek a trial, the very symbol of justice.

Lutze is found guilty. His punishment is to face precisely the suffering he caused. One by one, he is forced to endure the tortures to which he subjected the prisoners. The punishment is rooted in equality. The prisoners with their supernatural powers could surely have done worse, but are constrained by an internal ethos of fairness in process and punishment. As a result, Lutze is driven insane when local authorities find him in the camp, unable to see the ghosts.

A standard contemporary anti-Semitic stereotype is "the Jewish lawyer," a fast-talking shyster who manipulates others for personal gain. Serling, indeed, is writing in the post-World War II era when Jewish veterans made use of the GI Bill and attended college in overwhelming numbers. As a result, Jews rapidly moved into the professional class and adopted suburban lifestyles.[8]

It is stereotypical that Jews of this period sought out two professions in particular: doctor and lawyer. There is truth behind this stereotype. In Europe, from whence most of these Jews' parents emigrated, these were often the two professions that were open to them, others barred by anti-Semitic laws. To be a doctor or a lawyer was often the only way for a Jew to gain wealth and status in the old country cultures that otherwise sought to keep them impoverished. So, when the opportunity for advancement in the new country presented itself, these traditional routes were prized by the community as sure things. Hence, many Jews did become lawyers.

The job of the lawyer is to present arguments based on the intricacies and complexities of the law. This is easily coupled with the long-standing anti-Semitic trope of the Jew as bamboozler, as crooked bargainer in the marketplace. The result is the shyster lawyer. Of course, there would be some in any community and as a result of confirmation bias, every instance is used to justify the stereotype of the immoral, fast-talking Jew lawyer, which came to be commonplace in the culture, especially at this period.

In this episode, however, Serling has cleverly flipped that stereotype on its head. The Jewish propensity for law is not seen as the acquisition of power for the sake of self-enrichment, but rather as a commitment to legal structures that guarantee fairness. Lawyers are dedicated to a structure that gives everyone—even the most heinously guilty—the opportunity to have their "day in court," that is, to have their side of the story told and heard.

---

8. Brodkin, *How Jews Became White Folks*, 38.

In this way, the Jewish victims can be contrasted with their Nazi tormentor in their commitment to a system that guarantees justice for all, even those whom one dislikes.

This is a very Jewish approach. Jews are the "People of the Book." The Jewish God has no material shape, no form that can be represented as a material object to be worshipped as an idol. Instead, there is the Torah, a collection of words. Included in those words are 613 commands, the mitzvot, which Jews must obey, the Halakhic law. The law applies equally to all. Equality before the law is a Jewish contribution to Western culture.

But how does this law apply when the general truth of the law hits the complex contexts of the real world? It is true that "thou shalt not steal," but if you find a twenty dollar bill on the ground and put it in your pocket, are you stealing? Of course, it depends. If you saw someone accidentally drop it and they are a few steps ahead of you, then, yes. Putting that person's money in your pocket when you can call out and inform them that they just dropped their twenty would be theft. But suppose you are out on a walk and find it where there are no other people? You look around and see no one who might have dropped it and no one looking for it. Now, finders keepers. Congratulations, you are twenty dollars richer with a justifiably clear conscience.

This sort of thinking carefully about how the Halakhic law applies to lived experience is much of what is done in the Talmud, the commentary on the Torah, the other sacred text for Jews. The Midrash of the Talmud think carefully and cleverly about the meaning of the text of the Torah, looking for interpretation and insight in the same way one looks to Supreme Court opinions that seek to stay within the meaning of the law, but give insight into what it means in the real world.

So, there is both sociological and theological truth to the stereotype of Jews as lawyers. It is certainly the case that practicing law was seen as a good job and a way to secure not only wealth but status in the Jewish community of the late 1950s. But the practice itself calls back to the Talmudic scholar, the work that is seen as the most reverent and the most prized traditionally in the Jewish religion. Yet this picture of the Jewish lawyer is the opposite of that of the stereotype. This Jewish lawyer respects the law and sees interpretation not as self-serving but as justice-serving with the potential for moral insight. It was this sort of Jewish commitment to law that was exhibited by the ghosts of the victims of the Holocaust.

As such, Serling provides not only a disturbingly clear picture of Nazi atrocities in this episode, but also an underlying sense of Jews as committed to fairness and justice in a system that resembles that of America.

HE'S ALIVE

The last of the series of four episodes that focuses upon Nazism comes in the fourth episode of the fourth season, entitled "He's Alive," which was initially broadcast on January 24, 1963. It is the most explicit of the four episodes in terms of direct engagement with Nazism as a social phenomenon and a living threat. It can be seen as the capstone of the four-episode series.

Peter Vollmer (Dennis Hopper) is a young man from a poor, dysfunctional, abusive family. His father was a drunk who would beat him and Peter was becoming a juvenile delinquent with no future. His neighbor, a Holocaust survivor, Ernst Ganz (Ludwig Donath), becomes a father figure to him, a caring mentor who allows Vollmer to stay in his apartment when he needs to and provides insightful guidance to try to keep Peter on the straight and narrow path. Ganz's sympathy and care creates a bond of deep affection between the two of them.

Yet, because of his struggles, Vollmer searches for a scapegoat to explain his troubles. As a result, he becomes a White supremacist, forming a ragtag group in Nazi uniforms speaking out on street corners where they get mercilessly heckled by passers-by. This is an urban area just after World War II and the neighbors—many of whom are veterans, many of whom were patriotic supporters of the war effort, and many of whom come from diverse backgrounds—have little patience for these wannabe, cos-playing Nazis.

But then a figure appears who gives advice to Vollmer on how to speak, how to plan meetings, and what to do. The figure is either just off screen, shot from behind, or in shadow. We do not see the identity of the shadowy figure, but he speaks with great authority. He tells Vollmer that he must be made of steel for the movement to succeed. Every time Vollmer heeds his advice, the movement advances, crowds grow, Vollmer becomes more confident, more articulate, and more powerful. The advice always works.

As a result, the movement grows from street corner rants to organized meetings of larger and larger size. Vollmer begins to galvanize his crowds, who become more supportive of his hateful ideology. Banners, pictures, and other symbols are prominently displayed as the hall fills with more and more people who become more and more supportive of the message Vollmer conveys.

In the midst of this success, the shadowy figure tells Vollmer that his next move is to murder one of his inner circle, a boyhood friend who has been with Vollmer from the beginning and is entirely loyal. Shoot him in cold blood, Vollmer is told, and then blame the killing on the enemy. Make his friend a martyr to the cause. The crowd needs for the enemy to attack so that their cause is seen as all the more pressing. They need blood to get them to the next level.

Vollmer hesitates. He cannot murder his dear friend. But the shadowy figure demands it, for the sake of the movement and for the sake of Vollmer, who would trade in his soft humanity for steely commitment to the cause with this step. Vollmer eventually commits the crime and, as predicted, it elevates the anger and devotion of the crowd. Vollmer now has a dedicated Nazi following ready to start infiltrating the city politically.

It is at this point that Ganz, Vollmer's boyhood mentor, knew he had to act because he had seen this all happen before. When the Jewish owner of the local candy shop said, "That was another time, another place, another kind of people, that does not go here," Ganz responded, "That's what we said, too. They were brown scum, temporary insanity, part of the passing scene, too monstrous to be real. So, we ignored them or laughed at them because we couldn't believe there were enough insane people to walk alongside of them. Then one morning, the country woke up from an uneasy sleep and there was no more laughter." He decides that it cannot happen again.

Walking across the street, he mounts the stage to challenge Vollmer mid-speech. As Vollmer asks the crowd, "Do you want your homes infected with the vermin from foreign shores?" Ganz appears on stage behind Vollmer. As Ganz tells the truth about Vollmer, Vollmer pleads with him quietly to stop as the other neo-Nazis on stage demand that Ganz be taken care of. Vollmer, equal parts humiliated and conflicted because he knows what Ganz is forcing him to choose, tries to talk his mentor off the stage, but Ganz forces the issue. When Vollmer strikes Ganz in the face, Ganz replies, "The only kind of response your kind knows how to give," before leaving.

The encounter forced Vollmer to wrestle with the fact that those he was demonizing and dehumanizing were, in fact, people. The shadowy figure chastises Vollmer, tells him that he has the instincts of a rabbit, not a lion. When Vollmer demands that he step into the light, the figure does, showing himself to be none other than Adolf Hitler himself. The rise of Nazism is shown to be a formula that can be effective anywhere, even in America, even now.

In this cautionary tale, we find Peter Vollmer, a young neo-Nazi, humanized along the same lines as Serling's treatment of Lt. Mueller in the first of these episodes. But where Mueller is a sympathetic side character, this final episode focuses on the transition from fragile, damaged human psyche to heartless goon capable of killing those close to him. Hitler has Vollmer set up one of own his inner circle to be killed, the murder used to elevate the victim as a martyr to the cause, and Vollmer is forced to turn on his own mentor, Ganz, who directly confronts him publicly. Vollmer struggles at each step to rid himself of his humanity while Hitler angrily demands that he trade his human softness for steely commitment. But Serling's Hitler makes clear that there is a recipe, a simple set of steps that create nationalistic fascism. America may have defeated Nazi Germany, but it could very well be turned into it.

In this four-episode series, one episode per season for the first four seasons, that launched *The Twilight Zone*, we see Rod Serling responding to the central question of what it is to be a Jew in post-Holocaust America. If God had abandoned Jews in the ovens of Auschwitz, then it seemed only fair that some Jews abandoned God thereafter. Secular Judaism has flourished since the Haskalah, the Jewish Enlightenment of the eighteenth century when the scientific worldview coupled with the political emancipation of Enlightenment democratic norms gave educated, urban Jews a new approach to the world.[9] But it was after World War II that secular Jewishness took on a new challenge.

America in the 1950s turned Jewishness into Judaism. Wrestling with the Civil Rights Movement at the same time that Jews were assimilating, anti-Semitism was transformed from a form of racism into a religious-based bias among White people. Jews could be favorably contrasted with Black Americans by the racists as a model minority, as outsiders who were not trouble-makers, but who accepted the status quo as the status quo of the post-War boom that was being shaped in suburbia.[10]

Jews benefited from becoming insider-outsiders. But the echoes of the Holocaust led them to know in their heart of hearts that any embrace was not to be trusted. They may be insider-outsiders, but they were not and

---

9. Pelli, *Haskala and Beyond*.
10. Brodkin, *How Jews Became White Folks*, 130.

would never be insiders. They knew the oppression others faced and the brief respite from it—while the glare of hatred focused on others—did not excuse them from fighting against injustice. It was nice not to be the most hated group, but that did not mean they could avoid fighting hatred. Some, like Andrew Goodman and Mickey Schwerner, who were murdered with Black activist James Chaney by members of the Ku Klux Klan in Philadelphia, Mississippi, in 1964 for trying to register Black voters, knew it and paid the ultimate price for standing up for what was right.[11]

But it all left a sense of confusion in the Jewish mind of the early Cold War period. In the mainstream mind, Jewishness was reduced to Judaism, to be Jewish was to have a certain religious orientation. But what if you were irreligious? The notion of a secular Christian makes no sense. Christianity is a religion based on faith, accept Jesus into your heart as your personal savior and you are a Christian, don't and you aren't. But Jewishness is different. Judaism is a civilization, a tribe you are born into, one that does not hinge on the Greek notion of belief, but is something cultural, something deeper than mere religious faith or ritual. The anti-Semites knew this. Secular Jews were killed by the Nazis the same as those who practiced.

But this made no sense in the American context of the 1950s and 1960s. Secular Jews were Jews. They felt it. They knew the anti-Semites felt it, too. But they were excluded from the new categorization. What made them Jews? How could they express their Jewishness if the religious options were eliminated?

Rod Serling's answer to this question was to write. In these four episodes of the first four seasons of the *Twilight Zone*, we see an increasingly clear, direct, and emboldened attack on the hatred at the heart of Nazism, a hatred Serling knew was directed at him regardless of his conversion to Unitarianism, regardless of his agnosticism. It did not matter what he thought or believed, he was a Jew and it was thereby his obligation to oppose the sort of ignorance and hatred Jews knew all too well, no matter whom it was directed toward. It was that social-moral obligation that found you if you were Jewish and it was in these four episodes—and we will see, in others—that Serling expressed what it meant to be a secular Jew in post-WWII America.

11. Scheppler, *The Mississippi Trial*.

Chapter 3

"The Mighty Casey"

Striking Out Nazi Race Theory with Jewish Ethics

WHILE *THE TWILIGHT ZONE* contained explicit mentions of Nazism, as in the episodes discussed in the last chapter, more subtle, even covert attempts at undermining the intellectual foundation of Hitler's anti-Semitic racism can be found in the series. One example of a story that can be straightforwardly interpreted through a Jewish lens in order to subvert the theory of an Aryan master race and replace it with a more humane and Judaic sensibility is the thirty-fifth episode of the first season, entitled "The Mighty Casey," which was first broadcast on June 17, 1960.

The reference in the title, of course, is to the poem "Casey at the Bat" by Ernest Lawrence Thayer, written in 1888.[1] In the poem, Casey, a member of the Mudville Nine, is a batter of great power and confidence who comes to bat with the game on the line. The poem builds Casey into a heroic figure. The fans long for him to have a chance to hit, believing that his prowess would likely win the game: "If only Casey could but get a whack at that—We'd put up even money now, with Casey at the bat." Casey himself fully believes that his ability as a hitter is sufficient to guarantee a Mudville victory, "Then while the writhing pitcher ground the ball into his hip, Defiance flashed in Casey's eye, a sneer curled Casey's lip." Casey arrogantly takes two pitches which are called strikes, staking the entire game on his ability to hit the last pitch.

---

1. Thayer, "The Mighty Casey."

Thayer builds the tension at the climax of the story by stressing Casey's physicality.

> The sneer is gone from Casey's lip, his teeth are clenched in hate,
> He pounds with cruel violence his bat upon the plate;
> And now the pitcher holds the ball, and now he lets it go,
> And now the air is shattered by the force of Casey's blow.

Previously, we were witness to Casey's psychology, his cockiness and love of the limelight. Here, however, the focus has shifted with a change of bearing—from detached to violent. Now, we are focused on his strength as the bat exerts force on the surroundings.

The poem, of course, is a tragedy. The hero is brought down by his hubris.

> Oh, somewhere in this favoured land the sun is shining bright,
> The band is playing somewhere, and somewhere hearts are light;
> And somewhere men are laughing, and somewhere children shout,
> But there is no joy in Mudville—mighty Casey has struck out.

Casey, the baseball god is reduced to Casey, the mere human, the embarrassed loser, his bravado leading to his downfall and humiliation in front of all of his fans, who suffer heartache from his failure.

Serling's story is similar in that it too deals with baseball and the hopes of a team on the edge. The Hoboken Zephyrs are a terrible team, stuck in last place with no hope of advancing. They need to win the pennant, that is, to finish in first place in their division, to avoid being removed from the league altogether. The situation seems a sad, foregone conclusion as the team displays poor form in practice.

The Zephyr's manager, "Mouth" McGarry (Jack Warden), is approached by a mysterious Dr. Stillman (Abraham Sofaer) who has with him Casey (Robert Sorrells). Unlike Thayer's Casey, Serling's Casey is not a hitter, but a pitcher. Casey's fastball has shocking velocity and breaks the catcher's mitt. He is capable of throwing at superhuman speeds because Casey is not actually human, but rather a robot created by Dr. Stillman who is visually indistinguishable from a human, although he is good-looking, tall, strong, and blonde.

McGarry signs Casey onto the team and they win game after game on the strength of Casey's arm. Casey displays an oddly dispassionate nature, as one might expect from a robot. He does what is asked of him effectively, but always with a sunny yet detached disposition. He lacks the passion one would expect from a ballplayer; there is no joy in winning, no sense of aggression in competing. Casey simply does his job and does it well.

Eventually, Casey's true nature is discovered and the commissioner of the league (Rusty Lane) declares that Casey is ineligible. All appears lost for the Zephyrs until Dr. Stillman inquires what criterion, if satisfied, would allow for Casey to be considered human. The response is that a real human has a heart. Dr. Stillman replies that if possession of a heart is a sufficient condition, he is perfectly capable of making that adjustment, thereby allowing Casey to continue with the team.

After the procedure in which Casey is given a heart, he returns to the team. He looks the same and the commissioner and doctor's examination conclude that the sufficient condition of a heart has been met. Casey is once again on the Zephyrs, allowed to pitch. However, Casey is no longer successful. He has not lost his ability to throw with superhuman velocity, but now the batters are getting hit after hit against him, causing the Zephyrs to again lose every game.

When Casey is asked about his inability to strike out opposing batters, he explains that he is not incapable of getting the batters out, but rather that he is choosing not to. Now that he has a heart, he is able to empathize with the opposition, sees them as humans with hopes and dreams. When he strikes out an opposing player, he now realizes, he harms their ability to live the life they want for themselves. By allowing them to reach base safely, on the other hand, he is able to help them achieve their goals. He still has the arm, but because of his heart, he no longer has the will. Like Thayer's Casey, this Casey does not win; but unlike Thayer's Casey it is not hubris that brings him down but a sense of caring that elevates him to the status of a loser.

While it may not seem it, at first glance, this tale is very much an allegory of overcoming Nazism.

Among the most important and lasting propaganda works produced during the Third Reich is Leni Riefenstahl's *Olympia*. The 1936 Olympic Games were held in Berlin, three years after the election of Adolf Hitler as chancellor. They were seen by the Third Reich as both an international platform to elevate Germany's position in the world and also as an opportunity to demonstrate the truth of Nazi race theory, that is, the superiority of Aryans over members of other races. Richard Mandell, in his book *The Nazi Olympics*, writes, "The Olympic Games of 1936 were an important episode in the establishment of an evil political regime.... [M]uch of the success of the 1936 Olympics was due to the pursuit by the National Socialists of supremacy in mass pageantry. Hitler's success as a whole is inconceivable without the application of the contrived festivity that enveloped Nazism from beginning to end."[2]

That pageantry was not only documented but in important ways constructed by Riefenstahl in her film recording the event. *Olympia* is not reporting. We do not follow events the way one would on a modern telecast. Rather, the film documents the beauty of the games, especially the strength and allure of the human form.

This is part of Riefenstahl's aesthetic and was also present in her earlier work, *Triumph of the Will*, which was more explicit propaganda, documenting the Nazi Party Congress in Nuremberg two years earlier. Mandell comments, "Another quality of the film is its evocation of a Nordic Eros. Leni Riefenstahl had . . . a keen appreciation of muscular, male good looks. There are dozens of brief closeups of fine Aryan heads and shoulders."[3] The same holds true in *Olympia*, which is replete with such close-ups designed to frame masculine strength. This plays to an erotic sensibility that is not accidental as it plays a central role in Nazi mythology wherein the weak, the ugly, the disabled were less than human and the great, the tall, the strong, the able were more than human. What Riefenstahl provides in her artistic presentation of the pageantry of the games is less about the games and focuses instead on the obsession with physicality that was central to the National Socialist worldview.

The first shots of Casey on the mound that we see in "The Mighty Casey" clearly refer back to Riefenstahl. Casey is tall, handsome, and muscular. He is able to perform superhuman athletic acts. He is a god among men. We get Riefenstahl-style close-ups. We get wide shots that show his prowess. Casey is a constructed Aryan superman and he does what such a superman ought to do, he transcends by conquering the mere mortals who are his inferiors.

The Nazi notion of the superior being who asserts his will upon those who are lesser, thereby creating history has its origins in the writings of Friedrich Nietzsche. In his book *On the Genealogy of Morals*, Nietzsche famously writes, "At the centre of all these noble races the beast of prey, the splendid blond beast avidly prowling around for spoil and victory; this

---

2. Mandell, *The Nazi Olympics*, ix.
3. Mandell, *The Nazi Olympics*, 78.

hidden centre needs release from time to time, the beast must out again, must return to the wild."[4] The "blond beast" refers literally to a lion, but it is clear that the lion is itself a metaphor. Nietzsche is arguing that morality is a cultural artifact, established by those who possess the most political power.

Initially, that was the class he deemed "the Aristocrats," who were broad-chested and big-armed men who lived for the moment and sought only to satisfy their basest desires. These were men of short memory and little cleverness. They were men of action, of violence, of spirit, who took what they wanted, who climbed mountains because they were there, and who sought to do what had never been done to show that it could be done. For them, to call something "good" meant that it satisfied a want or a need. Food is good because you are no longer hungry. Drink is good because you are no longer thirsty. Sex or violence would be good if they brought about pleasure in the execution. "Bad" simply meant undesirable.[5]

The Aristocratic valuations do not include the concept of evil. Those who were unable to obtain the food, drink, or sex desired were not evil, but were not beings the Aristocrats wanted to be. It would be bad to be them. The Aristocrats did not hate the weak among them anymore than the eagle hates the lamb. Indeed, Nietzsche argues, the eagle loves the lamb because it is delicious.[6]

And, indeed, their lives were bad. They were hungry and beaten. To survive, they needed to develop something the Aristocrats did not have, memory. This would allow the weak to survive by hiding in the world of the strong. That memory was a double-edged sword, however. It not only allowed them to acquire a detailed understanding of places to hide, but forced them to relive the bad times. They remembered being hungry and having their food taken from them. They remembered being beaten viciously as the strong laughed at their inability to fight back.

This use of the memory created a mind that was now capable of all sorts of cognitive tricks, but among them is something that the Aristocrats lacked—hatred. The weak would hate the strong because of the torment to which they were subject at their hands, but even more so, the weak would hate themselves. The hatred turned inward and turned poisonous. This

---

4. Nietzsche, *A Genealogy of Morals*, 23.
5. Nietzsche, *A Genealogy of Morals*, 34.
6. Nietzsche, *A Genealogy of Morals*, 45.

generates what Nietzsche termed "ressentiment." This ressentiment tainted the soul of the weak and led them to brand the strong as evil.[7]

The cleverness of the weak allowed them to conceive of an imaginary Aristocrat stronger than any other, God, and armed with that concept they fomented a revolution, overthrowing the Aristocrats and seizing power. The Jews were the original priestly people who made this move.[8] The result of the revolution is a change in political power and therefore a change in morality, an inversion of morals, in which what had been good—triumphantly affirming your being by acting upon the world, meeting your physical needs and desires—became evil. Instead, morality was governed by "thou shalt not," by giving charity to the weak and needy, by helping those who are "less than." Now, one should feel guilty acting as the Aristocrats did and should repent. The slave revolt changed the world and introduced morality as we know it.[9]

This slave morality is a detriment to humanity, Nietzsche argued. It takes from the strong and gives to the weak. It thereby creates universal mediocrity. It disallows the great individuals from achieving their greatness. Humans make history by breaking history. We must destroy to transcend, but the new priestly morality prohibits breaking, discourages greatness, encourages only weakness among all. For humanity to advance, this slave morality and the ressentiment that it relies on, must be excised from the human soul. We must move beyond good and evil, reclaim our animal selves and be the great beings we could be. Only then will we evolve.[10]

It must, of course, be said that Nietzsche's thought was written in contrast to the system of Friedrich Hegel, who contended that history is a necessary process developing along a dialectic trajectory.[11] The individual is meaningless in the Hegelian system, only the whole is of value. Nietzsche is not a nationalist, but an individualist seeking to reelevate the metaphysical status of the individual. While the overtly anti-Semitic passages throughout Nietzsche's writings are manifest, he is not arguing that a master race should replace them. His writings were appropriated and misinterpreted

---

7. Nietzsche, *A Genealogy of Morals*, 52.
8. Nietzsche, *A Genealogy of Morals*, 34.
9. Nietzsche, *A Genealogy of Morals*, 34–36.
10. Nietzsche, *A Genealogy of Morals*, 56.
11. Hegel, *Phenomenology of Spirit*.

by the National Socialists to suit their political ends.[12] That being said, the influence is certainly there.

The Nazis did seek to manufacture through social engineering a superior brand of human being. They sought the great blond beast that would no longer live according to the dictates of the slave morality—thou shalt not steal, thou shalt not kill—but transcend them, to rise above and to take humanity to its next step of evolution.

We can see in the Casey of the first part of the episode—viz., the Casey without a heart—the successful realization of the Nazi program, the creation of a superior physical specimen who would have the ability to dominate ordinary humans with absolutely no conscience holding him back from greatness. Casey is the blond beast, his will is triumphant, he has made history though affirmation in his place as a superior athlete. The original Casey is the Nazi ideal of the Nietzschean *Übermensch*, the individual who overcomes the limitations imposed on society by Judeo-Christian morality.

But then Casey gets a heart. According to this telling, he ceases to be great. Now, he has become a slave to the priestly morality. The batters are inferior to him, yet he bows down to them, acquiescing to the needs of the lesser and thereby not being his best self, the great individual who had been making history by defeating them. The beast no longer takes his prey. It is unnatural.

This reading, of course, is clearly problematic. We see Casey as having become human and in the transition suddenly recognizing what it is to be a human and seeing it in others where he had not been able to see it before. This transformation just happens to be exactly the sort of thing described by the best-known philosopher of Jewish ethics, Martin Buber, in his best-known book, *I and Thou*.

Jewish ethics is fundamentally different from the standard Western approach, which is largely rule-based. There are true general ethical principles and an act is morally good if it is in line with those principles and morally wrong if it violates them. Some philosophers in the tradition, like John Stuart Mill, justify the rules in terms of consequences, that is, the true moral rules are those that when followed result in the best world.[13] Others, like Immanuel Kant, contend that reason itself justifies the rules, that certain acts are intrinsically good and others intrinsically bad.[14] Yet oth-

---

12. Kuenzli, "The Nazi Appreciation of Nietzsche."
13. Mill, *Utilitarianism*.
14. Kant, *Groundwork for the Metaphysics of Morals*.

ers, like Thomas Hobbes, contend that the rules are the result of a social contract that serves as the foundation for the culture.[15] Whatever the ultimate justification, the rules tell you how to and how not to act.

There are also rules in Judaism. The Torah has 613 commandments, called mitzvot, and they form the basis of Halakhic law, which sits at the heart of traditional Judaism. But these laws are not necessarily ethical. If someone does not keep kosher and eats pork, for example, that does not mean Jews think the person is a bad person. They think the person is a bad Jew. Unless the person is not a Jew, then *bon appetit*. The Halakhic law is the contract between Jews and God, not between people. The latter is what ethics is really all about.

Jewish ethics has the concept of hospitality, *hachnesat orchim*, at its core. When you see the stranger—that is, another person you have no connection to or reason to care about—the morally good person treats that stranger with hospitality. One can follow a rule to the letter and do it inhospitably. Think of the child made to apologize who says "I'm sorry" in a tone that expresses the opposite of contrition. The child did say the words that signify an apology, but they were not expressed in a truly apologetic way. The following of the rule does not mean that you have done what was supposed to be done.

The notion of acting hospitably implies that it is not rules, but *relationships* that ought to be at the center of ethical deliberation. A rule-based ethic has you consider the abstract, a hospitality-based ethic starts with you considering the other person. It is, at its foundation, a relational ethic.

Buber, then, begins by examining the sorts of relationships people can have with one another. We are capable of relating to other people the way we relate to objects, as tools for our own use. Buber terms this an "I-it" relation. "The I is not yet included in the natural, actual event which is to pass over into the primary word I-it, into the experience with its relation to I. The actual event is the separation of the human body, as the bearer of its perceptions, from the world round about it."[16]

Laura Mulvey, the feminist film theorist, for example, wrote of the "male gaze," which transforms a woman from a person into a mere object of desire. When men ogle at women in this way, it removes their humanity,

---

15. Hobbes, *Leviathan*.
16. Buber, *I and Thou*, 22–23.

their ability to be in an interpersonal relationship with the ogler, and becomes a mere thing, an "it."[17]

But there is another way to relate to others, what Buber calls the "I-thou" relation. No longer is the other person a mere object, but rather they are seen as a three-dimensional human with hopes, dreams, and dignity. When engaging in an I-Thou relation, the person recognizes their own humanity in recognizing the humanity of the other.

> If I face a human being as my Thou, and say the primary word I-Thou to him, he is not a thing among things, and does not consist of things.
> Thus human being is not He or She, bounded from every other He or She, a specific point in space and time within the net of the world; nor is he a nature able to be experienced and described, a loose bundle of named qualities. But with no neighbor, and the whole in himself, he is Thou and fills the heavens. This does not mean that nothing exists except himself. But all else lives in his light.[18]

When we make the move from I-it to I-thou, we treat the other with not only the respect that is due a person but also with care, a concern for them as a living project. A subject is something that has experiences. You are the subject of your life because you experience it. An object is a thing that you experience. We speak of "walking a mile in another's shoes," by which we mean that we can imagine what the other person's life is like, i.e., what it would be like to be a subject in their subjective reality. To move from I-it to I-thou is to recognize that the other person is a subject and not a mere object. We are never one, according to Buber, but in an I-Thou moment we occupy the subjective places of both, I am myself in experiencing my world as I do, yet in inhabiting the subjectivity of the other and seeing the world as they do I thus am also them during that instant. I am only me in an I-It interaction, but I am more than just myself when I have an I-Thou moment with another.

To some degree, we cannot help but have I-it relations with some people sometimes. For example, in the classroom, especially in universities where a professor might be addressing a lecture hall full of students, it is not possible for each student to have an I-thou relationship with the professor. The professor, for these students, is a mere tool, i.e., a knowledge-dissemination

---

17. Mulvey, "Visual Pleasure and Narrative Cinema."
18. Buber, *I and Thou*, 8.

machine and they are there to use the machine to increase their knowledge through attending the lectures.

But the idea is to try to maximize the I-thou relations where possible. The mail carrier delivers letters to your house. Take the time, when possible, to chat, get to know this person as a person, express gratitude. This is what a hospitable person would do. It is the morally right thing.

With this in hand, we can now reinterpret what was happing in the Casey case. When Casey had no heart, when he was a mere pitching machine, he himself was just a robot, a machine. He was not a Thou, not a subject. He did as he was programmed to do. He did not experience life, indeed he was not alive, he was only an object.

But when Dr. Stillman installed the heart, Casey was permitted to play because he was now a person. He had changed from being a machine, that is a mere object, into something a different category. Now he was a subject. Now he had a life. Now he experienced what he was going through.

At that point the batters changed as well. When he was a mere object, they were mere objects. But as soon as he became a subject, a Thou, he recognized the same in the other players on the opposing team. They were subjects. They had hopes and dreams. As a pitcher, he was placed in relation to the batter. As a human himself, he recognized the mutual humanity in them and thereby formed an I-Thou relation between the mound and the batter's box. This made him an ineffective pitcher, but a moral person.

So, what sense then do we make of this episode? Casey begins life as the ultimate realization of the Nazi project. He was tall, blond, handsome, and physically superior. He dominated the inferior and made history, standing above those he vanquished. Where the Nazi plan involved eugenics and social engineering, here there is a classic sci-fi *Twilight Zone* twist and mechanical and electrical engineering is used instead, but the end result is what Hitler dreamed of, an Aryan god who rose above mere mortals.

But then, Casey receives a heart. He becomes human and the transformation is complete, he goes from Aryan god to mensch. What happened when Casey the robot turned into Casey the person is that his fundamental relationship with others changed to one of hospitality. The Hoboken Zephyrs may be no more, but in place of them is the Jewish humanitarian ethic.

Chapter 4

Serling's Moral Inversion of Anti-Semitic Stereotypes

As a secular Jew who fought in World War II, Rod Serling saw it as his responsibility to make sure "Never again" was more than a mere slogan. We can see Serling's game plan against anti-Semitism as having two components, an offense and a defense. The offensive element in which he attacks anti-Semitism was to continually present before the public mind the horrors of Nazism and to make sure that Americans know that it could have happened here. This is what we see in the series of episodes from the first four seasons of *The Twilight Zone* discussed in chapter 2. Not forgetting requires constant reminding, which is essential for "Never again."

A different offensive tactic is appropriation. This is one way to interpret "The Mighty Casey," wherein the philosophical foundation of Nazi race theory was taken and re-envisioned through the moral lens of Jewish philosophy. In both cases, Serling could be understood as actively working to undermine anti-Semitic social movements and structures in order to assure that they would not blossom in the United States the way they had in Europe.

But Serling played defense, too, working to protect Jews from long-standing anti-Semitic attacks. America inherited the baggage of harmful stereotypes of Jews from the Europeans. Serling may not have directly experienced significant anti-Semitism himself while growing up, but it was all around him. Indeed, the period before World War II saw a swelling of anti-Semitic sentiment throughout America. A Jew walking into the subway in New York risked getting physically assaulted by members of the German

Bund.[19] Henry Ford had purchased the newspaper *The Dearborn Independent* for the express purpose of printing his overtly anti-Semitic screeds, forcing every Ford dealership in the country to circulate them.[20] On the radio, Father Charles Coughlin likewise spewed hatred for Jews, giving anti-Semitism an air of respectability by dressing it up in his clerical collar. Coughlin, for example, declared that *Kristallnacht*—the Night of Broken Glass when Germans rioted, looted, and murdered Jews with the tacit approval of the government—was legitimate and justified, focusing not on the death and damage, but on the wealth Jews had accumulated. His program was carried across the country and listened to weekly by millions.[21]

So, 1950s America was far from a blank slate for Jews. A range of preexisting stereotypical tropes had long propagated through the culture in such a way that in certain regions of the country Americans may have never met a Jewish person in their entire life, yet still had culturally acquired an image of them. And because of the long-standing Christian demonization of Judaism, that image was deeply negative.

Serling occasionally attacked that false visage head-on. We see that in the episodes previously discussed. In the hour-long episode "He's Alive," for example, the character of Ernst Ganz is clearly Jewish and displays both moral and heroic traits. He is compassionate, taking in and mentoring the young Peter Vollmer in his time of need. He is thoughtful in understanding the social dynamics and foreseeing the rise of anti-Semitic authoritarianism in America. He was brave in being willing to walk on stage, placing himself potentially in deadly danger, to speak the truth to those who least wanted to hear it, needing to have his voice heard confronting evil.

Similarly, in "Death's Head Revisited," the character of Alfred Becker, the ghost who accompanies Colonel Lutze and leads the trial, is also obviously meant to be Jewish. He is rational and deeply committed to justice and fair and honest procedure, rather than being hateful and burning for revenge. Like the rest of the spirits haunting the death camp, he is a Jew who embodies virtue . . . even while disembodied.

In both of these cases, we have Jews shown as heroic. One obvious path to undermining the negative images that the public already had is to try to replace them with stronger images they did not previously possess, but that are overwhelmingly positive in the fashion we usually understand.

19. Gartner, "The Midpassage of American Jewry," 262.
20. Ribuffo, "Henry Ford and the *International Jew*," 202.
21. Kolodny, "Catholics and Father Coughlin."

Jews, in this approach, are not the way the stereotypes portray them, but rather adhere to standard American virtues.

But Serling's primary approach to undermining anti-Semitism in the stereotypical understanding of Jews was, in fact, quite different. Rather than trying to undermine the stereotypical portrayals of Jews and argue that Jews were not at all like that, Serling created narratives in which the stereotypical tropes could be reinterpreted to be understood as positive traits. If the American population already connected certain properties with Jews, then let's show them that these are, in fact, affirmative qualities that should be celebrated.

ONE FOR THE ANGELS

Serling launches this strategy from the very beginning of the series with two episodes in the first season. In the second episode of that inaugural season, "One for the Angels," which was first broadcast on October 9, 1959, the main character is named Lew Bookman. The role is clearly coded Jewish. Consider the name. Not only does Bookman sound Jewish, but Jews refer to themselves as "People of the Book," so Bookman would make him one of those people.

Further, Jewish comedian Ed Wynn was cast to portray Bookman. Wynn, at the time, was widely recognized as a star of Vaudeville, Broadway, film, radio, and television. Lawrence Epstein, historian of Jewish comedy, wrote of Wynn, "His infectious giggle, his glasses on an expressive baby face, totally clean material free of suggestiveness or racial stereotyping, and use of costumes vastly amused audiences."[22]

During a golden age of Jewish American comedy, Wynn was thought of and often performed beside major Jewish comic figures like the Marx Brothers, the Three Stooges, Fanny Brice, Eddie Cantor, and Sophie Tucker. He was publicly known as yet another famous funny Jew.

But what really made the character of Lew Bookman Jewish was his occupation. The character is a pitchman, that is, he stands on the front steps of the courthouse in the middle of town with a random assemblage of wares trying to hawk them to random pedestrians passing by. This allows Serling to pack two of the standard stereotypes of Jews into the character, stereotypes that the audience would pick up upon from moment one.

---

22. Epstein, *The Haunted Smile*, 37.

The first is Jew as fast-taking hustler. Consider the anti-Semitic use of the term "Jew" as a verb. To "Jew" someone is to bargain in bad faith with the intention of selfishly extracting more than your fair share from the person with whom you are negotiating. The source of this term is the belief that Jews use language and cunning in the service of the greed that is endemic to members of the tribe. As a pitchman, Lew Bookman's entire line of work is to "Jew up" any and all passers-by.

The other stereotypical element is Jew as peddler. Since the middle of the twentieth century, when the GI Bill allowed the children of Jewish immigrants from Central and Eastern Europe to participate in the great wave of suburbanization, the stereotypical occupations of Jewish men are white-collar professions like doctor, lawyer, and accountant. But before this, going back a hundred years, the stereotype of the Jewish working man was the peddler carrying a sack full of assorted goods for sale. Indeed, in Europe and in nineteenth-century America expanding into the frontier, the Jewish peddler was not an uncommon sight.[23] Before railroads and dependable mail service, citizens of small towns and agricultural areas without access to the marketplace of larger metropolitan areas had a difficult time getting or replacing items necessary for daily life, from sewing supplies to cookware. The traveling peddler served these customers by bringing the goods to them. In areas where anti-Semitic laws kept Jews out of other jobs, this was one niche they could fill that would allow those with an enterprising spirit to improve their lot.

The character of Lew Bookman combines these two stereotypical Jewish elements with a Jewish name and a Jewish actor, thereby identifying his background to American viewers of the late 1950s using standard negative stereotypical properties. We were primed to not trust or like the main character.

Further, the episode opens with Bookman having a bad day. It is hot and absolutely everyone on the street walks quickly past Bookman, trying desperately not to make eye contact. Like contemporary telemarketers calling during dinner, the pitchman is an annoyance. We hate salesmen trying to sell us. They seem intrusive and slimy.

Serling begins the episode by invoking negative feelings toward a character designed to be thought of as Jewish, with standard stereotypical treatments of the day. As Serling puts it in the opening monologue, "Lew Bookman, a fixture of the summer, a rather minor component to a hot July,

23. Rohrbacher, "From Württemberg to America," 58.

a nondescript, commonplace little man whose life is a treadmill built out of sidewalks."

In the second scene, however, when the unsuccessful Bookman packs up his wares and heads home, we start to see that something is different. He is warmly greeted and interacts with the neighborhood children. They know him by name and welcome him home to his tenement apartment adoringly. After some chitchat, Bookman takes a windup toy robot he had been trying to hawk and gives it to the children as a gift. It becomes clear that this is not an unusual event, that the person we had been set up to dislike is, in fact, a very kind-hearted soul—generous, caring, and thoughtful. He may satisfy all the negative tropes we associate with Jews, but it turns out he is virtuous and lovable.

As our feelings change and we start to like Bookman, he enters his apartment and inside awaits an unexpected guest, the Angel of Death. In a twist on the Ingmar Bergman film *The Seventh Seal*, which was released only a year and a few months earlier, Bookman competes against Death for his soul. But it is not chess for Bookman. Death is convinced by Bookman to allow him to remain alive until he accomplishes his life-goal of making the world's greatest sales pitch, "a pitch for the ages, one for the angels."

Allowed to remain alive, Bookman rejoices until he realizes that Death has a quota. He must claim someone's soul to take back with him to the underworld. Just as Death finishes explaining these details, it becomes clear that the Reaper has chosen to fulfill his quota with Maggie (Dana Dillaway), the young girl to whom Bookman gave the robot, who has just gotten hit by a car outside Bookman's apartment. Bookman begs to be taken instead of Maggie, but his pleas are ignored as Death walks away.

The final scene opens at quarter to midnight on the stoop of Maggie's apartment, where the pediatrician tells Bookman the situation is unclear. Soon after, Death appears, saying he must claim Maggie's life at midnight for if he is not punctual with his appointments his entire schedule will be thrown off. With this comment, Bookman gets an idea: he sets up a sales pitch. Death laughs at Bookman, claiming he will get no sales at such a late hour. Bookman, shrugging off Death and confident in his abilities, begins regaling the empty street with descriptions of his fine products.

Despite originally laughing at Bookman's pitiful display, Death quickly finds himself enraptured by Bookman's pitch. He buys all of the items Bookman has for sale. With nothing left but his own body, Bookman sells himself as a personal servant to Death just as the midnight hour breaks.

With Maggie's life now secured by making Death miss his appointment with a sales pitch, Bookman has now completed his business and is ready to depart. They walk off together.

The Jew made the sacrifice, displaying the ultimate degree of selflessness for the sake of another. Bookman was responsible for the life of the girl. His obligation was to assure tomorrow by saving the girl in the same way that Abraham was shown to not lower the blade on Isaac, allowing Isaac to come down the mountain to create tomorrow.[24] The seemingly greedy, fast-talking Jewish peddler, once we got to know him well, turned out to be a thoroughly moral individual.

TIME ENOUGH AT LAST

We see another version of reclaiming Jewish stereotypical qualities later in the first season. The eighth episode, "Time Enough at Last," was broadcast on November 20, 1959. In it, the main character, Henry Bemis, is again an amalgam of stereotypical properties of Jewish men. First, he is a banker, and in the opening scene he is giving incorrect change to a customer. The assumption is that he is a cheat. The stereotype of the dishonest banker has long been associated with Jews.

It is certainly true that a number of the major investment banking firms in America were started by Jews. Although today when we think of Jewish American immigration we immediately bring to mind the Great Wave from the 1880s to the 1910s from Eastern Europe, there was a smaller trickle coming in decades earlier from Western Europe, especially Germany and Austria. These newcomers to America often started as peddlers and used their profits to create other businesses. Some, like Adam Gimbel and Lyman and Joseph Bloomingdale, built brick-and-mortar stores. Others, like Henry Lehman and Marcus Goldman and Samuel Sachs, used their money to move into banking. Jewish banks helped fund the rapid growth of the 1920's Gilded Age.[25]

But Jewish banking goes much farther back. In Europe, the lending of money for interest, usury, was frowned upon or outright outlawed by Christians. But credit is often necessary. Wars, for example, are expensive, having to pay soldiers, transport them, and purchase and repurchase arms and ammunition. In the midst of an armed conflict, it was not unusual for

---

24. Stern, *The Unbinding of Isaac*.
25. Supple, "A Business Elite."

the national treasury to run dry. Later, in the nineteenth century, with the launch of the industrial revolution, credit was needed to finance factories and other business ventures. Since Christians were not there to serve this essential financial function, Jews like the Rothschilds were more than willing. Doing so not only made them lots of money, but put them in proximity to the great power brokers of the Continent who were quite literally in their debt.[26]

As a result, it is a small anti-Semitic step to "Jewish bankers form a secret cabal who control the world leaders and therefore run the world." Father Coughlin said so explicitly during his broadcast, "We have lived to see the day that modern Shylocks have grown fat and wealthy, praised and deified, because they have perpetuated the ancient crime of usury under the modern racket of statesmanship."[27]

That step was aided by *The Protocols of the Elders of Zion*, a fake Russian work that claims to outline the surreptitious plot by Jews to assert invisible dominance over the entire globe.[28] It was promoted by Henry Ford, Adolf Hitler, and remains in circulation among anti-Semites today. It played upon and amplified the preexisting belief that Jews were immoral and greedy bankers who should never be trusted.

So, when Henry Bemis is shown to be a banker who gives incorrect change to a customer, Serling could be assured that a significant part of his audience would immediately peg the character as being Jewish.

Bemis was portrayed by non-Jewish actor Burgess Meredith and is shown to be short, weak, and wears extremely thick glasses. Another set of stereotypical traits associated with Jewish men is that they are physically feeble and passive.[29] Bemis is berated by his boss (Vaughn Taylor), a Christian who is a manly man and Bemis is seen as mousy in taking the abuse without fighting back. Indeed, the boss is not the only one who diminishes Bemis. We see him mercilessly mocked by his controlling wife. Jewish men as emasculated and hen-pecked again is a deeply ingrained stereotype.

The most revered member of a Jewish community is the rabbi, the scholar who spends time not laboring but hunched over the Talmud studying. As such, the traditional Jewish image of masculinity is not the strong,

---

26. Lottman, *The French Rothchilds*.
27. Weiss, *How to Fight Antisemitism*, 9.
28. Segel, *A Lie and a Libel*.
29. Abrams, *The New Jew in Film*, 91.

gallant, brave knight, but the smart, scrawny scholar.[30] That's not to say that there were not strong Jews, but such schleppers were seen as less manly precisely because of their muscles. Jews will often draw the racist distinction of *yiddische Kopf* (Jewish brain, which is clever and insightful) versus *goyische Kopf* (non-Jewish brain, which is slow and stupid). As People of the Book, intelligence and wisdom were prized and this created a basis for how a man ought to be. Indeed, you become a man in the community at your bar mitzvah, literally "son of the law," by reading from the Torah. It is engagement with the Book that makes you a man and you are made more manly through deeper and more profound engagement with it.

In the hands of anti-Semites, this difference in the picture of masculinity becomes instantiated in Jewish men being non-men. Jews are, if not gay, effeminate and ineffective. Jews are wimps, unable to occupy the position of dominance saved for a real man of the Christian mold.[31] Bemis is weak, subservient to a woman, and physically incapable. This very much conforms to the traditional anti-Semitic stereotype of Jews.

Finally, Bemis is single-mindedly obsessed with reading: fiction, the newspaper, or poetry, he adores the printed word in all its forms more than anything else in life. Jews, again, are referred to as "People of the Book," and bookishness is yet another stereotypical aspect.[32] Like Lew Bookman, then, Henry Bemis is an amalgam of traditional anti-Semitic stereotypes, albeit a quite different set of them.

The episode follows poor put-upon Bemis living a miserable life, getting cut down at work and at home. He is continuously bullied. His enthusiastic love of reading leads his wife and boss to absolutely forbid him from finding pleasure—clearly the only pleasure he has—in texts. But, as Jews are stereotypically portrayed (as they are, for example, in Wagner's Ring Cycle and Nietzsche's *Genealogy of Morals*), they use their wits to hide from power. And so, Bemis does, hiding in the bank vault at work in order to read. It is a solitary place where he can be alone.

But it is also a place with impenetrable walls. Just as the lunching Bemis reads about the hydrogen bomb, World War III is launched, destroying all human life on earth. But because of the security of the vault, Bemis is saved, rendering him the last man on earth.

---

30. Boyarin, *Unheroic Conduct*, 2.
31. Boyarin, *Unheroic Conduct*, 97.
32. Abrams, *A Lie and a Libel*, 35.

He wanders about, panicked at first, trying to figure out how he will survive. Finding food in the ruins of a grocery store, he knows he will eat. But then, he makes the discovery that shows that he will not only survive, but thrive. He comes across the remains of the public library and its almost unlimited store of books. What might seem like hell has transformed into heaven. Bemis excitedly creates great piles of books, figuring out the order in which he will read them, undisturbed in his literary paradise.

Until, of course, his glasses fall from his face and his lenses break. It is one of the great ironic plot twists in television history, rendering the story simultaneously a comedy and a tragedy.

The end feels tragic because we have become empathetic toward Bemis. As we did with Lew Bookman, we began with a sense of antipathy. Both characters began as stereotypical Jews and the small snippet of everyday life in which we were first introduced to the characters psychologically primed us to have negative feelings toward them. But as the episodes progressed and we came to know the characters better, we developed affection and sympathy for them. This is Serling's defensive approach. Instead of admitting that the stereotypes are morally problematic and arguing that real Jews don't fit the stereotype, he instead humanizes those who do. Of course, not all Jews have the stereotypical profile, but if we can defuse the stereotype it would not matter.

It should be noted that both the cases of this redemptive stereotyping involved male characters. The lone stereotyped female character, Helen Bemis, is explicitly not given the same humanizing treatment. Played by Jacqueline de Witt, who was not Jewish, the character does embody the cliched property of being domineering that is often attributed to Jewish women.[33] But instead of being humanized, Helen remains a flat cartoon whose negative properties were amplified from merely being controlling to being downright dastardly and sadistic. When, for example, Henry picks up one of his favorite books of poetry, he opens it to find that Helen took a pen and blacked out all of the words to deprive him forever of the joy of reading it.

Unlike his treatment of stereotypical properties for Jewish men, there were no other female characters in the series who received anything like the humanizing treatment given to Lew Bookman and Henry Bemis. Serling's writing for the series in general tended to feature male characters. Only a

---

33. Antler, *Talking Back*, 243.

tiny minority of episodes penned by Serling contain female characters in significant roles.

While this sort of sexist weighting was common for the era, a separate factor is that Jewish women had fewer specifically Jewish stereotypes to contend with (as if the general misogyny of the times was not enough). The European notion of *la belle juive*, the Jewish female as the embodiment of temptation and bodily sin luring otherwise virtuous Christian men away from their faith and wives,[34] never really became part of the American collective mind.

The image of the Jewish mother, on the other hand, was to some degree present in the culture. Indeed, it was given exactly the sort of treatment that Serling gave to Bookman and Bemis in the radio and television character of Molly Goldberg, written and portrayed by Gertrude Berg, in *The Rise of the Goldbergs*. But to Americans away from the urban northeast and cities of the West Coast, even that archetype would not have been deeply penetrating. The incorrigible Jewish mother and the spoiled, self-centered Jewish American princess would not become standard American cultural archetypes until the end of the 1960s,[35] after the complete run of the initial version of *The Twilight Zone*.

IN PRAISE OF PIP

As is the case in "One for the Angels," the episode "In Praise of Pip," which first aired as the initial episode of the fifth season on September 27, 1963, wrestles with a Jewish stereotype that would have been identifiable at the time, but has since waned in the cultural mind, that of the Jewish mobster.

In the story, Jewish actor Jack Klugman portrays bookmaker Max Philips, who lives a clearly problematic life. We meet him in his room where we learn that he is not only a bookie—one who makes illegal bets, in Philips's case on horse races—but also an alcoholic. We begin with the glimpse of a dark life, that only gets darker. A baby-faced young man named George (Russell Horton) walks into Philips's room to confront him about a $300 bet that George had placed with Philips, and lost on, the day before. Philips convinced George, whom he is close enough to call "Georgie Porgie," to bet on a long shot with money that he stole from his job. When the horse lost, something Philips seemed to know would happen and shows no remorse

---

34. Abrams, *The New Jew in Film*, 69.
35. Prell, "Why Jewish Princesses Don't Sweat," 75.

on having conned George over, George finds himself facing a future in jail and begs Philips for help. Philips seems heartlessly unmoved by the appeal, arguing that life is an ugly place.

When Philips is giving over his week's con-money to the head of the gang (Saul John Launer), we learn that Philips's envelope is $300 light. Philips is confronted about not taking the bet from George, who is then brought with black eyes into the room by the boss's henchman (Kreg Martin). Philips appeals for the young man, but is told that if you make a bet and don't pay up, this has to happen to maintain the violent integrity of the gang.

The American mythology around organized crime has been driven largely by films such as *The Godfather*, *GoodFellas*, and *The Untouchables* and the long-running series *The Sopranos*, which feature almost exclusively Italian Americans as the central figures. When asked to name a famous gangster, those brought up on media representations will quickly reach for an Italian name like Al Capone, Lucky Luciano, or John Gotti.

But the fact is that from the 1920s through to the time of *The Twilight Zone*, Jewish organized crime was just as influential and just as violent. Abe "Kid Twist" Reles ran the Brooklyn-based group known as Murder, Inc., while the Dutch Schultz mob (Schultz's real name was Arthur Flegenheimer) controlled much of Manhattan. Chink Sherman, Schultz's enemy, had a foothold in Boston, while Shondor Birns terrorized Cleveland and the Purple Gang, run by Abe Bernstein, did the same in Detroit. Perhaps the most-remembered Jewish gangsters of the time, Benjamin "Bugsy" Siegel and Meyer Lansky, oversaw a synthesis of Jewish and Italian mobs into a nationwide crime outfit called "The Syndicate."[36]

The most notable artifact of the Syndicate was the transformation of Las Vegas, Nevada, from a sleepy little town just a short drive away from the Hoover Dam, an engineering marvel and tourist attraction, into America's adult playground. The original casino/hotels were opened and run by locals, but with the rapid expansion of Los Angeles and automobile travel along the interstate highway system, organized criminals realized that there would be a sizeable appetite for a "sin city" within a day's drive. They built what has come to be known as "The Strip," a stretch of what was Highway 91, now Las Vegas Boulevard, populating it with legendary, but now demolished, hotels like The Sahara, The Sands, and The Riviera.[37] The first of

---

36. Fried, *The Rise and Fall of the Jewish Gangster in America*.
37. Land and Lord, *A Short History of Las Vegas*.

them was The Flamingo, whose construction and operations were overseen by Bugsy Siegel, that is, until he was discovered skimming the profits and was murdered for it.

In the late 1950s and early 1960s, at the time of *The Twilight Zone*, Vegas was entering its heyday, represented by the Rat Pack of Frank Sinatra, Dean Martin, Sammy Davis Jr., and Joey Bishop—the first two were Italian American and the last two were Jewish. But the shining neon lights, the sparkling sequins adorning half-dressed showgirls, and the spotlight on famous singers and comedians never completely eclipsed the dark side of Las Vegas. The quickie wedding and divorces, the drinking, and especially the gambling were always there providing the edge that Las Vegas possessed. In addition to slot machines and table games, there were the sports books, betting on athletic events, the lines of which were set by bookies, many of whom were Jewish.[38]

As such, the character of Max Philips, his line of illegal work, his callousness toward life, and his ability to talk people into doing things they should not do and otherwise would not have done was very much in line with another sort of Jewish stereotype of the time.

But as with the other cases, we see a humanization. The episode begins with a disconnected scene at a frontline surgical hospital in Vietnam, where a soldier named Pip is brought in with life-threatening injuries. A surgeon says that he likely will not make it. In the next scene, we see on Philips's nightstand a picture of a young boy and a picture of a young soldier. Pip is Philips's son.

A later scene places Pip in a proper hospital where his operation has just been completed by a medical team. The head surgeon tells the assistants that if Pip can survive the hour there is a chance he could pull through. He wishes the resting Pip good luck.

During the surgical procedure, Philips is in his boss's office with the henchman and the badly beaten George when he receives news of a telegram telling him that Pip has been badly hurt in the war and may not pull through. Looking through the window at an adjacent amusement park, Phillips reminisces about how much young Pip loved the park and how much he regrets having been a bad father.

As focus returns to George, it becomes clear that they intend to murder the young man and Philips pulls a knife to defend him. In the fight that

---

38. Fried, *The Rise and Fall of the Jewish Gangster in America*, 120.

follows, the gangsters are both stabbed, Philips is shot in the abdomen, and he sends George away free. Philips has defended the vulnerable.

He staggers out to the gate, and in an explicitly religious moment, Philips prays to God, asking for one last chance to talk with Pip. The gate of the amusement park opens for him and he walks in to see a ten-year-old Pip. The lights on all of the rides and games suddenly turn on. The critical hour that may be Pip's last is to be spent with Philips, as they relive their most joyful time. Cotton candy, the Ferris wheel, and the shooting gallery allow them both to be together one last time. At the end of that hour, Pip, disappearing into the hall of mirrors, informs Philips that he, Pip, must go now. Heart-broken and panicked, Philips searches in vain for Pip among the false reflections.

Pip gone, Philips staggers, holding his bleeding wound back to the front gate, where he once again addresses God, offering his own life, if it would save that of his son. In the final scene, we see Pip, limping in uniform and using a cane, as he enters the amusement park remembering his father.

The plot is an inversion of the story of Genesis 22, the binding of Isaac. While Jewish commentators meditate on multiple meanings of the story,[39] the standard understanding in the Christian world, and therefore the one most present in the minds of the audience of *The Twilight Zone*, is that God visited Abraham and told him to sacrifice his son as a test of Abraham's faith. He complied and his hand, wielding the knife was stopped when the test was successfully completed. We famously find this understanding, for example, in the writing of Søren Kierkegaard.[40]

In "In Praise of Pip," we find the story turned on its head. Instead of a righteous man who passes a test by willingly sacrificing his son, here, instead, we find a man who failed the test by living a morally flawed life and who finds absolution through a last selfless act of sacrificing himself for his son. Of course, it was not out of character for Philips to be self-sacrificial. We may have begun with the stereotype of the nihilistic, self-interested, violent street Jew, but we saw Philips's care for George and his lifelong love for his son. We learn of the soft heart beneath the hard exterior.

As with the earlier cases, Serling starts us off with a pat stereotypical portrayal of an implicitly Jewish character. But what exposes itself as the episode unravels is that the stereotype needs to be inverted, the true

---

39. Stern, *The Unbinding of Isaac*.
40. Kierkegaard, *Fear and Trembling*.

understanding of the human being inside of the stereotype is, in fact, that he is a good person.

A PASSAGE FOR TRUMPET

This was not the only time that Serling used Jack Klugman in this way. A more complex version can be found in "A Passage for Trumpet," which was first broadcast on May 20, 1960, as episode thirty-two of the first season.

Although the portrayal of Mrs. Bemis in "Time Enough at Last" might be understood as exposing gender as a blind spot for Serling, the concerns around race in America certainly was not. Indeed, one can see Serling's commitment to the civil rights struggle as interconnected in Serling's mind with his opposition to anti-Semitism. It is only in America, after Jews assimilate, that Jews were not considered racially different. In Europe, Jews were commonly—not only by the Nazis—considered racially distinct from the general population. This held in America as well until Jews had largely assimilated. Jewishness was not reduced to Judaism until the twentieth century and so the Black struggle for equality could easily be sympathetically seen by a secular Jew like Serling at the time.

Recall that before *The Twilight Zone*, Serling tried twice to bring to the small screen dramas based on the brutal murder of Black teenager Emmett Till and the failure of a corrupt system to bring his murderers to justice. Because of overt racism in America, he was censored in dramatizing Till's murder when trying to produce both "Noon on Doomsday" and "A Town Has Turned to Dust," his teleplays that sought to capture the injustice of Till's killing and the acquittal of his racist killers. He found that the only way he would be allowed by the network and the sponsors to tell a version of the tragic story was by changing central elements, including an unproduced attempt to make the victim Jewish.

The alterations hid the influence of Till's story, but the veneer was thin enough that it could be seen through. Today, we would see this as morally problematic appropriation, of one people stealing the suffering of another. But at the time, it was the only way that the secular Jew, Serling, could do what he felt he needed to do to serve the cause of civil rights. The need for this sort of racial camouflage in putting social-justice-based themes on television was a lesson he would bring to *The Twilight Zone*.

In "A Passage for Trumpet," jazz trumpeter Joey Crown, played by Klugman, is a talented performer who has lost his job because his alcoholism and substance abuse has made him unreliable and hampered his ability to play with depth. Fired from his standing gig, he winds up down and out. When he has to pawn his beloved trumpet, Crown sees his life as over and decides to commit suicide. However, just as he has stepped in front of a truck, he finds himself in a provisional afterlife accompanied by a guardian angel, Gabriel (another clearly religious reference), portrayed by John Anderson, who knows Crown well. Together they discuss life and art and what it meant to perform improvisational music and to relate to other people. Given the opportunity to return to the world of the living, Crown changes his mind and returns to his old life, now having survived getting hit by the bus.

Jews were no strangers to jazz. From Benny Goodman, Artie Shaw, and Tommy Dorsey to stars of the late 1950s like Stan Getz and Buddy Rich, it would not have been unusual for a Jew to be a professional jazz musician.[41] However, the stereotype of the troubled jazz genius whose work was undermined by their addiction was not one generally associated with Jews. With figures like Billie Holiday and Charlie Parker, the story of Joey Crown was playing on a stereotype of African Americans that inhabited the mainstream culture at the time.[42] Serling was again substituting a Jewish figure in the place of a Black character, but doing so in the same way that he did with Lew Bookman and Henry Bemis.

When we meet Crown, he is at his worst, confrontational and violent—again negative aspects of the stereotypical "angry Black man." As was the case with Bookman, Bemis, and Philips, Serling plays on our familiarity with the stereotype and its negative cultural connotation to prime us to see the main character as an anti-hero. But through the episode, as we delve deeper into the psyche and soul of Crown—again, just as we did with Bookman, Bemis, and Philips—our connection to the character evolves. We become sympathetic. Crown is humanized and we root for him.

One can understand Serling's reticence to use Black actors as he does Jewish actors in the instances of stereotype inversion. He is Jewish. This gives him greater latitude to work with, and to work against, in order to undermine Jewish stereotypes. Further, the time of *The Twilight Zone* was, again, a time of assimilation and social, cultural, and economic advancement for many Jews. Jews were in a safe enough place that this sort of intellectual move could be made.

41. Hersch, *Jews and Jazz*.
42. Singer and Mirhej, "High Notes."

It was very much not the case with Blacks in America. This was a difficult period. Church bombings, lynchings, and connections between politicians, law enforcement, and groups like the Ku Klux Klan were a reality. The struggle was for the basic rights of citizenship and treatment as humans under the law.

Serling was sensitive to this and as a result, we see Black characters in *The Twilight Zone* not portrayed in stereotypical ways, something highly unusual for the times. Indeed, unlike with the above-mentioned Jewish characters, Serling's Black characters are notably distanced from stereotypical presentation.

When Serling wrote Black characters into episodes of *The Twilight Zone* care was taken to explicitly avoid what were seen at the time as racially archetypal elements. Their dialogue, for example, is free of the sort of dialect or accent that was often present in the usual racially tinged portrayals.

This is even true when surrounding White characters did speak in explicitly regional accents. In the season 5 episode "I Am the Night—Color Me Black" first aired on March 27, 1964, a White citizen named Jagger (Terry Backer) is about to be hung for having committed murder. He shot to death a local member of the Ku Klux Klan during a physical altercation and it comes to light that facts that might have allowed the condemned man a viable self-defense alibi were hidden by the sheriff (Michael Constantine) and the local newspaper editor. Further, the deputy, who was present at the scene, and clearly allied with the Klansman, perjured himself in the trial. The deputy, played by George Lindsey (best-known for his portrayal of Goober on *The Andy Griffith Show*), has an explicitly southern drawl, despite the fact that the setting is noted several times as being in the Midwest.

The townspeople are united in their excitement over the hanging. They want blood.

Yet, something strange happens on the morning of the execution. The sun has not risen. The town is completely in darkness. The surrounding towns see daylight at the usual hour, but this town remains dark.

In front of the gallows, Black actor Ivan Dixon (best-known for his role as James Kinchloe in *Hogan's Heroes*) portrays the Reverend Anderson, who speaks with the condemned man just before the execution and declares him guilty. When the condemned man tells the reverend that he is taking the easy way out by siding with the majority, the reverend defends his position until after the hanging, when he realizes that the hatred in all of their hearts is the poison causing the darkness.

The role of Reverend Anderson is a complex one. The character is both of the people and above the people, intellectually and spiritually superior, but undergoing growth throughout a single pivotal scene with profound dialogue and monologue. There is explicit reference to race in the conversation with the accused, but it is not the focus of the discussion. In 1964, however, the notion of cultural hate could not be disentangled from the racist violence directed at the Black communities where the civil rights struggle was at its most urgent. The character's blackness is made distinct from the obvious whiteness of the overwhelming majority of the rest of the townspeople, but is not emphasized in the way blackness often was represented on television at the time.

We see this as well in another episode starring Dixon, "The Big Tall Wish," which premiered on April 8, 1960. In this episode, Dixon plays Bolie Jackson, a washed-up boxer who tries for a comeback. He has befriended Henry (Steven Perry), the son of his single-mother landlady (Kim Hamilton), and is clearly good to the boy, taking him to ballgames and for walks in the park.

In his comeback fight, Jackson is confronted by a crooked White fight promoter (Walter Burke) and in anger from the promoter's taunts punches the wall (instead of the promoter) and breaks his right hand just before the fight, causing him to lose the bout terribly. But as he is being counted out, Henry makes a wish and the boxers magically switch places, with Bolie becoming the winner of a fight he dominated instead of having been dominated. Only Bolie and Henry know what happened, but Bolie refuses to believe in the magic and this ends up reversing the wish.

In the episode, virtually the entire cast is Black with the exception of the promoter and Bolie's corner man (Charles Horvath). The apartment is located in a Black neighborhood and Bolie interacts with people on the street. Again, there is no dialect or the sort of racial markers that were common in portrayals of Black life in the late '50s/early '60s. Serling explicitly strips any sort of stereotypical elements out of the representation. Indeed, what we see is the opposite, where he is careful to morally contrast the Black and White characters, with the White characters engaging in ethically problematic behaviors and the Black characters as morally superior.

While Serling is clearly trying to undermine both Jewish and Black stereotypes, he does so using quite different techniques. For his Black characters, he creates straightforward good humans with no hint of the stereotypical elements. It is a sort of argument by omission. We can undermine the racist vision of Blacks in America by showing them to simply be normal, good people.

With respect to Jewish stereotypes, on the other hand, he takes a different and more interesting approach. Serling writes the characters of Bookman, Bemis, and Philips in a way that we understand to be coded Jewish, making use of negative stereotypes initially. By the end, each episode humanizes the characters so that the viewer comes to like them as good people. Serling shows that the lot of Jews is difficult—Bookman, Bemis, and Philips live lives that we do not envy—but despite their difficult circumstances, they are caring, gentle, thoughtful, morally good individuals. Serling is intentionally coupling anti-Semitic stereotypes with pro-Semitic portrayals.

In the shadow of the Holocaust, in a US where Father Coughlin and Henry Ford mainstreamed hatred of Jews, Serling used his platform to both show the dangers of Nazism and the virtues of Jews in order to try to reshape the cultural narrative in a fashion that allowed American Jews to live in safety.

Chapter 5

The Borscht Belt Meets Orion's Belt

Jewish Comedy in *The Twilight Zone*

THERE IS NO DOUBT, as we have seen, that anti-Semitism and Nazism were topics of concern to Rod Serling, as they were every other Jew of the generation that witnessed, much less fought in, World War II. But Jewish culture is not just obsessing about genocide. No, it is obsessing about genocide while eating and making jokes. *The Twilight Zone* is primarily remembered for its fantasy and science fiction content, but there were comedy episodes as well. The brand of comedy we find in them should be understood in terms of the changing phases of Jewish comedy that could be seen in American culture at the time.

Comedy is deeply rooted in the American Jewish tradition. A couple decades after *The Twilight Zone*, a study conducted by Samuel Janus found that 80 percent of professional comedians were Jewish, despite Jews only making up 3 percent of the American population at the time.[1] That is an absurd domination of that corner of the entertainment world. Scholarly and popular treatments of Jewish humor—including Joseph Telushkin's *Jewish Humor: What the Best Jewish Jokes Say about the Jews*, William Novak and Moshe Woldocks' *The Big Book of Jewish Humor*, Joseph Dorinson's *Kvetching and Schpritzing: Jewish Humor in American Popular Culture*, Ruth Wisse's *No Joke: Making Jewish Humor*, and Jeremy Dauber's *Jewish Comedy: A Serious History*—look for the source of this connection between humor and Judaism, in Jewish religious rituals, symbols, and ways of thinking.

---

1. Janus, "The Great Comedians," 171.

But many of the great Jewish comedians were secular. True, some like George Burns and Jack Benny, came from Orthodox homes,[2] but many others came from secular backgrounds with little education or interest in Judaic matters. Jewish humor comes not from the shul, but from the culture. Secular Jews, like Rod Serling, were just as funny, if not more, than their practicing counterparts. If we want to find the roots of Jewish American comedy—and the dominance of Jews in comedy, especially at that time, is a particularly American phenomenon—then we need to think about the Jewish American experience. Art reflects life and comedy is an art form. The sort of comedy made at a particular moment tells us about the people who made it.

The Twilight Zone appears at a turning point in Jewish American life, when Jews are leaving the urban tenements and menial jobs for suburban homes and white-collar professions. Jews were still living in the shadow of the Holocaust, yet with their sudden elevation on the socioeconomic ladder, they were slowly becoming seen not as a different race, but merely as a different religion. They were still outsiders, but less so. As such, we expect to find changes in Jewish American comedy that reflect this, and we do. However, *The Twilight Zone*, in laying at the vertex of the angle taken by the social trajectory of American Jews, will have comedy reflective of the different eras that border it.

There has been American Jewish comedy as long as there have been Jews in America. The early immigrants from Germany and Vienna gave us print cartoonists like Milt Gross and Rube Goldberg. The Great Wave of Eastern European Jews fleeing the pogroms and May Laws from the 1880s to the mid-1910s, brought their own performers with them and established the Yiddish Theatre, which included everything from melodrama to comedy. Stars like Sigmund Mogulesko, Menasha Skolnick, and Molly Pincon generated huge laughs, making room for the next generation of comic actors like Fyvush Finkl.[3]

The children of these immigrants grew up on the lower East Side of Manhattan during the roaring '20s. Many lived in crowded, disease-ridden, dangerous tenements in dire poverty, working in sweatshops. Yet only a few blocks away they saw tremendous wealth. These Jews had imported European-style social democratic ideals that led to a strong trade union movement. The American labor movement resented these immigrants,

---

2. Burns, *Gracie*, 64; Benny, *Sunday Nights at Seven*, 46.
3. Kanfer, *Stardust Lost*.

believing that they were taking away jobs from "real Americans," so Jews formed their own unions, which gave rise to social banks, collective health insurance, and newspapers like *The Daily Forward*.[4]

This sense of an unfair economic structure causing hardship in day-to-day life would inform the antiestablishment nature of the comedy that Jews of this generation created. The Three Stooges, the Marx Brothers, and the Ritz Brothers attacked the well-to-do by wreaking havoc on representatives of the status quo. Irving Howe explained this ethos in terms of the films of the Marx Brothers:

> In their films the disassembled world is treated with total disrespect, an attitude close to the traditional feeling among Jews that the whole elaborate structure of gentile power is merely trivial. The gleeful nihilism of the Marx Brothers made a shamble of things, reducing their field of operations to approximately what a certain sort of East Side skeptic had always thought the world would be: *ash und porukh*, ashes and dust.[5]

The non-Jewish world has built an intrinsic structure. As Jewish social philosopher Herbert Marcuse put it:

> The prevailing forms of social control are technological in a new sense. To be sure, the technical structure and efficacy of the productive and destructive apparatus has been a major instrumentality for subjecting the population to the established social division of labor throughout the modern period. Moreover, such integration has always been accompanied by more obvious forms of compulsion: loss of livelihood, the administration of justice, the police, the armed forces. It still is.[6]

Jewish liberation and economic justice seem to require a complete dismantling of the constructed system and Jewish comedians of the period were doing their part.

Then came the Holocaust, following a period of rising anti-Semitism, not only in Europe but in America as well. High-profile figures like Henry Ford and Father Charles Coughlin were pushing Jew-hating conspiracy theories into the mainstream.[7] Jews were both unpatriotic communists trying to undermine the values of the country and power-crazed capitalists

---

4. Dawidowicz, "The Jewishness of the Jewish Labor Movement."
5. Howe, *World of Our Fathers*, 567.
6. Marcuse, *One-Dimensional Man*, 9.
7. Ribuffo, "Henry Ford and the *International Jew*"; Warren, *Radio Priest*.

whose moguls controlled the media and whose bankers controlled the governments.

It was no longer safe for Jews to make comedies that attacked the structure, that sought large scale social changes in the name of economic justice. Jews needed a much lower profile. As a result, the character portrayed in Jewish comedy switched to the *schlemiel*, the weak loser for whom nothing ever seems to go right.[8]

On the radio, there was George Burns, who became one of the first mainstream characters to regularly see a psychiatrist at a time when mental illness was seen as a weakness. Jack Benny would be put down by Mary Livingstone, a woman, and Rochester, his Black valet (much to the distaste of Southern audiences).

Jews seeking to vacation were not welcome at most hotels, so they opened their own, a string of resorts across the Catskill Mountains widely referred to as "The Borscht Belt" where a new brand of Jewish comedy developed that launched the careers of some of the biggest names in comedy.[9] Jewish men were wimps, brow-beaten by their wives. Perhaps the most well-known of them was Henny Youngman, who made jokes like, "My wife wanted a fur coat and I wanted an automobile. So we compromised, she got a fur coat, but we keep it in the garage."[10]

Jews felt vulnerable and the consequences of arousing the suspicions of the majority were crystal clear (or perhaps, *Kristallnacht* clear). As a result, Jewish humor changed its tone. While the character lived on in the works of Woody Allen, Richard Lewis, and Larry David, the tone once again changed once Jews began to assimilate and gain social capital as they came to be considered more White.[11]

Two strands of Jewish comedy developed at the end of the 1950s and beginning of the 1960s. On the burgeoning new medium of television, Jewish comedians like Milton Berle, Sid Caesar, and Phil Silvers portrayed much more muscular characters. They were brash. They were tough. They could give it and take it. Male Jewish comedians could once again be real men.

On the other hand, because the GI Bill had sent so many Jews to college, a headier, more sophisticated strand of Jewish comedy began to

---

8. Epstein, *The Haunted Smile*, 55–128.
9. Adams, *The Borscht Belt*.
10. Youngman, *Take My Wife, Please*, 60.
11. Stratton, "Not Really White."

emerge from the halls of the nation's top universities. Harvard gave us the sardonic song parodies of Tom Lehrer and Berkeley gave us the improvised rantings of Mort Sahl, creating a more intellectual brand of comedy for the post-WWII modern lifestyle.

Rod Serling's comic episodes of *The Twilight Zone* find themselves at the inflection point between these three phases: the weak schlemiel, the muscle Jew, and the partially assimilated modern Jew. Serling not only pulled from each of these movements, he did so by casting some of the biggest rising names in Jewish comedy associated with them.

MR. DINGLE, THE STRONG

In the nineteenth episode of the second season, "Mr. Dingle, the Strong," the plot centers on a weak little wimp named Luther Dingle who is a vacuum salesman and all-around loser. In a neighborhood bar, he comes across a bully whom Serling describes in the opening narration as "every anonymous bettor who ever dropped rent money on a horse race, a prize fight, or a floating crap game, and who took out his frustrations and his insolvency on any vulnerable fellow barstool companion within arm's and fist's reach."

The scene plays out the way one would expect, with the bully picking on Dingle, pushing him around and humiliating him in front of the bar's other patrons. Then comes *The Twilight Zone* twist when a two-headed Martian scientist endows Dingle with superhuman strength. Dingle thrashes the bully, giving him his comeuppance. Realizing what he can now do, Dingle parlays his new power into wealth and fame, becoming arrogant until the Martian scientists, their sociological experiment now complete, become Delilah to Dingle's Sampson, taking away his strength just before he is to demonstrate it on live television. The final punchline is that on their way out of the bar to return to Mars, the alien scientists meet up with colleagues from Venus, who decide to see what would happen if they did to Dingle's brain what the Martians did to his body, making Dingle a super-genius.

We see Serling once again playing with two standard Jewish stereotypes: the weak schlimazel and the tough, gambling street Jew. Where in the episodes discussed in the previous chapter, Serling's goal was to undermine these stereotypes by humanizing the characters so-typed, here he is simply using them to set up a gag. The use of stereotypes in this way is commonplace. Think of every ethnic joke. If a priest, a blonde, and a German walk into a bar, you know exactly who the characters in this very short story are. No more needs to be said to establish the active properties of the individuals whose words and deeds will comprise the content of the joke.

Luther Dingle is played by Burgess Meredith, who occupied a similar role as Henry Bemis in "Time Enough at Last." The unnamed bettor, on the other hand, is played by a *Twilight Zone* newcomer, Don Rickles. Known as "The Merchant of Venom" or "Mr. Warmth," Rickles was one of the leading insult comics of his era. After getting out of the Navy—another young Jewish man serving during World War II—he trained as an actor at the American Academy of Dramatic Arts, where a number of his classmates, like Jason Robards, Tom Poston, and Grace Kelly, went on to great stardom as serious actors.[12] Rickles tried comedy, doing strange conceptual pieces that could have been straight out of *The Twilight Zone*, such as a skit in which Peter Lorre had a head made of glass.[13] These bits did not go over well and Rickles was failing as a comedian.

That is, until one day as the entertainment at a bar mitzvah when he was getting no laughs. Annoyed, he asks the bar mitzvah boy, "Is this your father? What happened? Did a bus hit him?" The crowd loved it. He continued, "Is this your mother? What does she see in your father?" Roars of delight. "I'll be honest, this crowd looks like a real mercy mission. So just give me the kid's gifts and let me go home early." A huge wave of applause. People liked being insulted by Don Rickles. He never looked back.[14]

When his father died, Rickles moved with his mother to Miami Beach, where she befriended the mother of Frank Sinatra. When Sinatra came down to play in Miami, Rickles's mother asked if Frank could see her son's act. Mrs. Sinatra said that of course he would. Frank Sinatra may have been a tough guy who was famously quick to use his fists and refused to be pushed around, but he listened to his mother.

When Sinatra walked into the little club where Rickles was performing, his massive entourage in tow, the whole room stopped watching the show and turned to gawk at Frank Sinatra, the biggest star of the day. To reclaim the audience's attention, Rickles said, "Make yourself comfortable, Frank, hit somebody." Everyone froze. Sinatra was infamously sensitive about being the butt of jokes. But then Frank started to laugh, at which point everyone started to laugh.[15] Because their mothers were close, Sinatra

---

12. Rickles, *Rickles' Book*, 30.
13. Rickles, *Rickles' Book*, 48.
14. Rickles, *Rickles' Book*, 56–57.
15. Rickles, *Rickles' Book*, 64.

considered Rickles to be his little brother and that came with the privilege of busting on each other—indeed, Sinatra's practical jokes on Rickles were often much worse than anything Rickles said about Sinatra on stage.

With Frank Sinatra in his corner, Rickles became a regular in Las Vegas and started to pick up roles in the movies. In "Muscle Beach Party," "Bikini Beach," and "Beach Blanket Bingo," he played the bad guy.[16] This was the Don Rickles that we see in Serling's comedy. The rough Don Rickles, the nasty comedian, who has the tables turned on him by a little nebbish who got help from Mars.

THE MIND AND THE MATTER

We see range in Serling's comedy pieces with the twenty-seventh episode of the second season, "The Mind and the Matter," which first aired on May 12, 1961. In this piece, Archibald Beechcroft is an urban professional working in an office full of people in a city full of people, and Beechcroft hates them all. A young man named Henry (Jack Grinnage) at work tries to befriend Beechcroft, but turns out to be a klutz and spills coffee on Beechcroft. As an apology, he gives him a copy of a book called "The Mind and the Matter," which Henry claims can teach Beechcroft ways to change the world.

Initially skeptical, Beechcroft takes the book and reads it. Using the techniques he learns from the book, Beechcroft realizes that he is capable of making people disappear. At first, he rids himself of specific troublesome individuals, but then he realizes that he can cause large groups to vanish and ultimately clears the entire city of the rest of its population, leaving him completely alone.

At first, Beechcroft enjoys the solitude, no longer having to deal with the people who so bugged him normally. But eventually, the loneliness begins to mess with his mind. His own reflection seems to be mocking him. He realizes that he cannot survive in a world by himself.

But if the world was to be repopulated, he thought that it would be best not to return it to the crowds of annoying others. Instead, if he had to have company, he would want others like himself. So, he recreates the urban population, except that every single person in the entire city is Archibald Beechcroft.

A city full of curmudgeons turns out as badly as one would imagine. So, Beechcroft learns his lesson and returns the world back to the way it

---

16. Rickles, *Rickles' Book*, 101.

always was. As he steps in the elevator, he sees Henry, who once again spills coffee on Beechcroft's suit. Asking about the book, Beechcroft ends the show with the punchline, "Totally unbelievable."

The part of Archibald Beechcroft was played by Shelley Berman. Berman was born in Chicago, where he trained as an actor.[17] Moving to New York, he found little work, as he got nervous during auditions, so he returned to Chicago, where he joined a troupe called "The Compass Players," named after the bar "The Compass," whose back room they used as a black-box theater.[18]

The Compass Players were directed by Paul Sills, the son of Viola Spolin, a theater professor at the University of Chicago who developed the improv games that all actors today use in their training.[19] Sills was taking Spolin's philosophy and seeing how it could be applied beyond mere exercises. Initially, the Compass Players would improvise entire productions, each scene having a predetermined starting and ending point and the actors having to get from one to the other collectively without a script. Eventually, they switched to short-form improvisation where groups of actors would create scenes. The Compass Players would eventually rebrand themselves as "Second City" and become the troupe that created some of the biggest names in comedy, including David Brenner, Robert Klein, Joan Rivers, and much of the original cast of *Saturday Night Live*.

While it was still the Compass Players, however, Berman joined. He learned a lot and was doing well when he decided to split from the group with two other actors to form their own three-person team. Eventually the other two, Elaine May and Mike Nichols, decided that they would split off on their own[20] and went on to stardom, at first as an improvisational team and then later individually as actors and directors.

Berman was left to decide what he wanted to do when he saw stand-up comedian Mort Sahl at the great Chicago nightclub "The Gate of Horn." Sahl was a revolutionary in the field, taking a newspaper on stage and riffing on the day's news, giving insightful commentary as he mocked the powerful. He was not telling traditional setup/punchline jokes, but doing something more improvisational. It was a new sort of combination of what

---

17. Epstein, *The Haunted Smile*, 183.
18. Sweet, *Something Wonderful Right Away*, 27.
19. Sweet, *Something Wonderful Right Away*, 11.
20. Nesteroff, *The Comedians*, 170.

Berman had been doing with The Compass Players, but different in that it was a monologue.

Mentored by Sahl, Berman created a different sort of approach, perfect for him, one more theatrical, less political, but more personal. Where Sahl took on big ideas, big people, and big problems, Berman focused on the small, the mundane, the sort of thing everyone can identify with. Berman played a modern everyman, stuck in the sort of uncomfortable messes we all find ourselves in but try to hide from the rest of the world. He created what we now call "observation comedy," where you point out things that everyone knows, but look at them from a slightly different angle, showing them not to be normal, but absurd. That style would be perfected in the 1990s by Jerry Seinfeld and Larry David, which is why when David needed to cast someone to play his father on his post-*Seinfeld* show *Curb Your Enthusiasm*, he chose Berman, who artistically was very much his symbolic father.

Berman's most famous bit, captured on his first album, the top-selling *Inside Shelley Berman*, has Berman playing a man in an office who looks out his window to see a woman holding onto the ledge of the skyscraper department store across the street and having to make his way through the maze of the phone chain in the department store to get the right person to rescue the woman. As he is transferred from department to department—and back to the original departments—he gets frantic while trying to keep his cool. The frustration of the impotence of the modern person generates the absurdity and the laughs.

The role we see Berman play for Serling is precisely the same. Berman's office worker in his own work is entirely reminiscent and comedically similar to what Serling wrote in "The Mind and the Matter." It was very hip, urbane comedy at the time which very much matched the style of Berman. Unlike the brand of comedy that Serling wrote for Don Rickles, which was much more raw, the style of comedy for Berman was more intellectual and modern.

CAVENDER IS COMING

"Cavender Is Coming" is the thirty-sixth episode of the third season of *The Twilight Zone* and starred the well-traveled Jewish comic character actor Jesse White (best-known as the lonely repairman from a long-running series of advertisements for the washing machine manufacturer Maytag and also well-known for his portrayals of multiple historical figures in the satirical album *Stan Freberg Presents the United States of America*) and soon-to-be comedy legend Carol Burnett. Despite the fact that it aired third of the three episodes to be discussed, its roots in Jewish comedy go back the farthest, playing on a traditional class-based incongruity, but doing it twice, one contained inside of the other like Russian nesting dolls.

The initial mismatch is the framing of the plot in which Harrison Cavender—the caricature of the hard-drinking, cigar-smoking street Jew—somehow ends up in Christian heaven, where he is being considered for inclusion among the angels. Where other cherubic candidates pass the entrance exam easily, it is not so for Cavender and he is given one last chance to use his magical powers as a guardian angel to improve the life of an unfortunate schlemiel on earth.

The unfortunate loser Cavender is assigned to help is Burnett's Agnes Grep, a kind-hearted klutz, "put on earth with two left feet, an overabundance of thumbs and a propensity for falling down manholes," as Serling puts it in the introductory narration. We first meet Grep as she fails in what is clearly the most recent of a long string of jobs, this one a movie theater usher. The other women in the position are competent, graceful, and smooth, whereas Grep is nervous, awkward, and unable to get the words out of her mouth. Her misdeeds escalate until they climax with her falling down a flight of stairs and crashing through a mirror, ending up on the ground in her boss's office, where she is fired.

On the bus ride home she meets Cavender, who has to convince Grep that he is, indeed, her newly assigned guardian angel. In a classic series, he transforms the bus into a horse and buggy, into a sports car, and then back into the bus. After arriving home to her low-rent apartment, the best she can afford as she is unable to hold down a job, and having to relive the day's misadventure with her neighbors, the second incongruity is introduced into the plot.

Cavender changes Grep's life completely, making her fabulously wealthy. To assure that he succeeds and becomes a full-time angel, Cavender pulls out all the stops and gives Grep a fortune, a mansion, and all of the trappings that go with an upper-class life. "As of this moment," Cavender tells Grep, "you are independently wealthy." She has new friends, the sycophantic hangers-on who tend to surround wealth. She has persistent gentlemen callers. Her weekly games with her bowling team are replaced with upscale parties, the first of which Cavender conjures.

Leaving Grep to enjoy her new life at the party, Cavender does what the irresponsible Cavender would do, magically creating for himself the best martini he ever drank and then magically creating more of them, getting himself drunk at the party.

The next day, Grep leaves her mansion and returns to the apartment building of her old life, where the people she loves do not know her. Instead of improving her life, Cavender's actions have alienated Grep from all the things she held dear. Despite the fact that all of her problems seemed to be fixed by the wealth Cavender created, Grep is no happier and asks that her life be restored to the way it was. Cavender complies with the wish.

Returning to heaven, Cavender is deemed a failure until his superior looks down at earth and finds that Grep is indeed happy, happy with the simple life she has always had. Returning from her misadventure in high society, Cavender tells her that she has "an abundance of wealth," she was always rich—rich in friends, rich in love, and rich in the sort of authentic elements wealth cannot buy. This insight is enough to make Cavender's travails on earth an accidental success and he becomes a full angel. In the closing shot, Cavender pulls out a cigar and puts it in his mouth.

To devotees of the history of Jewish comedy, Cavender's cigar bookended at the beginning and end of the episode bring immediately to mind the Marx Brothers. Indeed, "Cavender Is Coming" can be seen as an homage to the Marx Brothers and classic Jewish comedy of the interwar era. During this period, the Marx Brothers, the Ritz Brothers, the Three Stooges, as well as figures like Fanny Brice and Sophie Tucker played on the same incongruity, take American Jews who were the children of immigrants—poor, uncouth, and untrained in the ways of proper society—and put them where they do not belong. In the case of the Marx Brothers, the settings of their films was always some place you would never expect to find lower-class recent immigrants: a Florida luxury hotel (*The Cocoanuts*), a country estate (*Animal Crackers*), a cruise ship (*Monkey Business*), a university (*Horse Feathers*), government leadership (*Duck Soup*), and an opera company (*A Night at the Opera*). Putting proletarian immigrants in a bourgeois setting, the clashes of manners become unavoidable and from that incongruous hilarity ensues.

The characters played by Groucho Marx were always those of a poor Jew trying to con his way into high society, often by courting the character played by Margaret Dumont, who was invariably a wealthy, WASPy widow.

Groucho's character did not belong in the world of Dumont's character and donned a façade in order to remain there as long as possible.

But no matter how hard he tried to maintain the false front, he was undermined at every turn by the characters of Chico and Harpo, who were fellow immigrants unable to wear the same sort of mask. Where Groucho's character was identifiable to audiences of the time as Jewish, Chico's was Italian and Harpo's was Irish, making the three of them representative of the major waves of immigrants who came in through Ellis Island at the time. The result was cultural conflict that created the Marx's brand of zany comedy.

The character of Cavender is very much in line with the sort of approach seen in the Marx Brothers and thereby very much in line with one of the major threads in Jewish American comedy writ large. Take a streetwise, rough-edged stereotype of a particular kind of Jew well-known to audiences and then introduce him into a polite Christian setting where he does not belong and allow the incongruities to create situations where the mismatch becomes funny.

In "Cavender Is Coming," then, as well as in "Mr. Dingle, the Strong" and "The Mind and the Matter," we see the comedy in *The Twilight Zone* very much in line with the range of approaches we see in the various threads of Jewish American comedy at the time. Indeed, the range of approaches we see from Rod Serling is reminiscent of the changes seen in Jewish American comedy in the period of the late '50s/early '60s, including silly slapstick and more hip, modern, intellectual approaches. But in all of it, there are the fingerprints of the American Jewish experience.

Chapter 6

Three Rabbis Named Chaim
Neo-Talmudic Television

ROD SERLING: IMAGINE, IF you will, the hit 1990's program *Mystery Science Theater 3000*, except that instead of a human and two robots making wisecracks about B movies, we now have three rabbis all named Chaim discussing six episodes of *Twilight Zone* as Talmudic midrash.

The Torah contains 613 mitzvot, blessings or commands that are taken as laws from God that Jews are called upon to follow, but like any written laws, they are so general that they require interpretation for particular contexts. That interpretation is provided by classical rabbis in the form of the midrashim of the Talmud, sacred hypotheticals designed to help us understand how to perform our obligations, whether they be to God or others, within the specifics of lived life.

Judaic ethics requires being for the Other, which, in turn, requires understanding the needs of that particular Other in their particular circumstances, but because of the multiplicity of human possibility, a single mitzvah can generate many midrashim helping us understand how to act in any given moment, no matter how unusual. Talmudic Judaism, a house of midrash, drives this understanding into Jewish homes, the public sphere, and beyond.

Thus, to be ready for whatever lies ahead, rabbis continually discuss the midrashim, looking at the many interpretations in order to understand how the same law applies differently with new information in a wide range of cases. You must prepare yourself, as Franz Rosenzweig taught, for the unplanned encounter. Through study and practice, you learn how to behave when called for help. Study, practice, and experience readies one, the ordinary person, for the tasks at hand.

This, too, is what was being done in *The Twilight Zone*, where the program's ethical teachings function midrashically, addressing the same command in different contexts, asking the same question about obligatory ethics at both personal and political levels, but in different situations in different episodes.

Consider, for example, the Talmud-Torah obligations for hosting the stranger, a very Jewish requirement, as there are more commands on being hospitable to and for the stranger than any other biblical injunction. There are different kinds of strangers: strangers in our midst, such as houseless people, people observing other traditions, prisoners of war, as well as nomadic strangers who come, but not with an intent to stay. As the early Hebraic community had settled down and began to farm the land, encounters with strangers were a regular and potentially explosive situation, with nomadic strangers passing by with an intent to take and leave. The Israelites were called upon to remember that they too had been strangers in Egypt before the exodus and therefore they should hospitably engage those who came by.

One can imagine modern contexts in which this would be problematic behavior. For example, suppose the stranger is a Nazi pretending to be Jewish. What are your obligations in this case? *The Twilight Zone* challenges the Torah/Talmud obligation to be hospitable to the stranger with multiple different cases in which earth is visited by nomadic strangers or humanoid aliens who are human enough to be engaged with, but far enough away to be Other.

Despite the fact that the humanoid aliens seem in need of a host, in some of these episodes they find the converse to be true. The alien is the host. How does one avoid the misplacement of trust in a bad stranger or bad host while being a good host? Should one begin with distrust after being burned or does one start over with trust when encountering a new stranger? From the destruction of Solomon's Temple to the massacre at the Tree of Life synagogue in Pennsylvania, Jews all over the world are experientially aware that their places of gathering and worship may be targeted by the violence of Jew-haters. Are synagogues and temples to trust any person who comes to them for worship or help? How does one host a person who triggers communal distrust while finding out if they are really who they say they are?

To answer those questions, we must study and practice. And that is exactly what our three rabbis named Chaim are doing, while watching . . . *The Twilight Zone*.

PEOPLE ARE ALIKE ALL OVER

First broadcast on March 25, 1960, as the twenty-fifth episode of the first season, the plot opens with two astronauts traveling to Mars. After the optimistic pilot Warren Marcusson, played by Paul Comi, dies as a result of damages received from the ship's crash landing, his crewmate Sam Conrad, portrayed by Roddy McDowall (who ironically would go on to play the converse role of Cornelius in *Planet of the Apes*) fears interacting with an unfamiliar species and is left to fend for himself. As the Martians begin to tap on the ship and even find a way to open the hatch, Conrad panics and grabs a gun in self-defense.

When Conrad sees the Martians, however, he lets his defenses down, realizing that the aliens have a humanoid form and appear to have peaceful intent. Conrad then proceeds to tell of his purpose for journeying to their planet. The Martians ask the astronaut to remain in his ship while accommodations are made for him.

In the next scene, the Martians bring Conrad to living quarters eerily similar to that of earth. With Conrad satisfied with his accommodations, the Martians leave. Conrad soon thereafter realizes that his new place of residence is not just a home, but a jail cell: there are no windows, the doors do not open. When Conrad rips down the tapestry in the living room the walls slide open to reveal an audience of expectant Martians. Confused, Conrad shouts at the Martians in hopes of getting an explanation. A revelation comes in the form of a sign that reads, "Earth Creature in His Native Habitat." Conrad has been placed in an intergalactic zoo.

This midrash broke the rabbis' heart. Why did they go to Mars? What was there? What did they need? Did Mars have it? How did going to Mars help anyone? Why would anyone go there? Why would anyone presume they'd be welcome there?

[Rabbis Chaim 1, 2, and 3 enter with Rabbi Haayim]

Chaim 1: How was golf with Rabbi Haayim 2?

Haayim: Awful! The group in front of us was more than slow. They wouldn't let us pass.

Chaim 2: It's Wednesday; the blind pastors play on Wednesday.

Chaim 3: How could you not tell?

Haayim: They can't play at night?

Chaim 3: Is there popcorn?

Chaim 2: Chava made some.

Chaim 3: Excellent! [To Haayim] Where are you going?

Haayim: To play an evening round with Rabbi Chaim 4.

Chaim 1: We have to discuss.

Haayim: Really?! No such thing as TV midrash.

Chaim 2: Chava made popcorn.

Chaim 3: [Offering the popcorn to Haayim] Without salt, but enjoy. Sit.

Haayim: You're not going to come to any legal conclusions.

Chaim 1: True. We're not searching for Halacha (legal rule). But prophetic understanding matters, especially when it comes to Nazis.

Haayim: Prophetic life is no match for Nazis. If they're coming, I'm playing one more round.

Chaim 2: You should go take care of your family if they're coming.

Chaim 1: Do you reject the *Pirkei Avot* (Ethics of our fathers)?

Haayim: I don't need to watch TV to study the *Pirkei Avot*. [Leaving] I'll be part of better discussions playing golf. TV isn't Torah with midrashic programming.

Chaim 2: Take some popcorn.

[Haayim leaves.]

Chaim 1: I'm not berating Conrad for misunderstanding, that's my every day, but to ensure we don't make the same mistake. He lacked the "know how" to ethically prepare for this. The needed self-reflection and vigilance against being only for himself was beyond his reach. He wasn't ready for those he didn't know. He never asked: "How do I prepare myself for the stranger I don't know is coming?"

Chaim 3: You can't. No one can prepare for this.

Chaim 2: You can, we know not to make it about ourselves. We know how to be vigilant in making it your reflex.

Chaim 3: Still doesn't prepare you for the unexpected.

Chaim 1: We can have tools for the unexpected, but we can't know what hasn't happened. "Don't listen to your arrogance" is one tool.

Chaim 2: That's what I'm saying.

Chaim 3: It's not what you said.

Chaim 1: Going to Mars came from their arrogant, selficating conduct, acting little differently than the Martians.

Chaim 2: They're ugly, kind of like Nazis, but Conrad's cowboy colonialism put him in their hell.

Chaim 3: It's telling us we can't be like Martians. The midrash resists treating one another like objects or things. Conrad wasn't a thing, nor a fan favorite, but he wasn't something to grab, take, or consume.

Chaim 1: They're responsible for him?

Chaim 3: For his well-being.

Chaim 2: What does that look like?

Chaim 3: Sending him home would be a good start. They caged him for the sake of their world. He was no more than a thing for their consumption. A mere thing. And "thing can never be presented personally and ultimately has no identity. Violence is applied to the thing: it seizes and disposes of the thing. Things give, they do not offer a face. They are beings without a face."[2]

Chaim 2: Denying him the freedom to respond robbed him of a home.

Chaim 3: He doesn't have a home. Without the opportunity to respond, he can't make a home. There's no shared space for discussion.

Chaim 1: There is no greater disease than the loss of hope.

Chaim 3: Conrad is Serling's lesson to overcome our "selficating" habits, living at the expense of the Other and subsequently ourselves. Hearing only what one wants to hear can put the whole community at risk.

Chaim 2: He murdered it; selficating responses can be murderous.

Chaim 3: Yeah, don't be like him. Selfication offers no resistance to Nazis.

Chaim 1: What does?

Chaim 2: Speaking falsehoods into reality cost Conrad his life. My tongue dies when I don't hear the Other, the lights go out. As Rosenzweig told us, there is no monologue before dialogue.

Chaim 3: Conrad was like a Jew to the Nazis, an object that could be caged, studied, and discarded.

HOCUS-POCUS AND FRISBEE

Our next midrash is "Hocus-Pocus and Frisbee" from season 3, episode 30, first broadcast on April 13, 1962. Frisbee, played by Andy Devine, is one of the most extraordinary men in the world. Although he is in his sixties and runs a general store, Frisbee gained a PhD in meteorology at thirteen, discovered a one-hour travel route from Paris to Berlin, and is a master with computers . . . or so he likes to say. In reality, Frisbee is a teller of tall tales, who gets a kick out of sharing his fictional adventures with his friends at the store.

In the middle of one of his myriad tales, two men pull up asking for gas. At first, Frisbee tries to tell a story about how he invented the rear-engine automobile, but is perturbed by the men's odd behavior. Although still kind, Frisbee focuses on conducting business rather than friendliness.

Later in the evening, Frisbee hears a strange voice calling to him. The voice beckons Frisbee to go on an adventure and head to a field beyond a highway. Although Frisbee refuses, instead opting to make dinner, Frisbee is nonetheless forced into the adventure, as he is magically transported to a spaceship. Frisbee, believing the ship to be a movie prop, climbs on to find the mysterious men he served back at the gas station. The men reveal that they are actually aliens and want to bring Frisbee back to their planet as the paradigm of humans, having become aware of Frisbee's innumerable achievements. Frisbee, realizing that the aliens have taken the tall tales at face value, attempts to explain the notion of lying. Unperturbed by Frisbee's comments, the aliens force Frisbee to stay on the ship.

In the next scene, Frisbee, out of remorse over his captivity, plays a song on the harmonica. Unaccustomed to the sound of a harmonica, the aliens freeze in agony. Realizing that he can use the harmonica to his advantage, Frisbee continues to play music and escapes the ship while the aliens lay on the ground paralyzed. Frisbee then returns to his home, to find his friends have set up a surprise birthday party. When Frisbee's friends lovingly ask him to tell one of his fantastical stories, Frisbee relays his adventures with the aliens. Frisbee's friends quickly shrug off the story as another tale of fantasy, despite claiming to have been honest this time around.

Chaim 1: Lucky guy.

Chaim 3: Unless the joke is on us. He was thrown to them, but like a Frisbee, they threw him back. He was no cowboy, but he had a harmonica.

Chaim 2: Music can resist fascism.

Chaim 1: Not always.

Chaim 3: You like Wagner?

Chaim 2: There are people I like who play him. Frisbee was unabashed. It's why they threw him back. Conrad betrayed community, Frisbee created it. Music is shared.

Chaim 3: Music isn't always shared as Frisbee shared.

Chaim 1: He still should have done more listening before boarding the ship. Frisbee had a lucky throw.

Chaim 2: It wasn't luck that made him loved by his community. Frisbee is fun and fun is hospitable, just like his name and harmonica.

Chaim 1: He assumed what he gives to others will be given to him.

Chaim 2: Playing harmonica showed he hadn't lost sight of home. Perhaps he was trying to harmonize with the aliens?

Chaim 3: That had nothing to do with them. Lesson is to listen and not end up there.

Chaim 1: Lesson is to also not lose sight of yourself. Frisbee was being Frisbee when he played the harmonica.

Chaim 2: Frisbee ended up at home.

Chaim 3: He's not Ulysses. He wasn't the same person who flew back home.

Chaim 3: Sure, he was. He was never for the aliens, but for his community. He returned to himself, not like Ulysses, but like Joseph when reunited with his brothers.

THE LITTLE PEOPLE

In season 3, episode 28, first broadcast on March 30, 1962, "The Little People," follows astronauts William Fletcher (Claude Akins) and Peter Craig (Joe Maross), who make an emergency landing on a desolate, desert-landscaped planet after their spaceships start to experience technical failures. Captain Fletcher focuses on survival and ship repairs, while Craig, a man with aspirations of power, laments his situation without helping.

While exploring the planet, Craig discovers a society of microscopic people. The aliens direct him to sources of fresh-water and food. Using his comparatively large stature, Craig decides to play out the role of the tiny people's god. After observing Craig has an unusual amount of water in his canteen, Fletcher demands to know about Craig's mysterious disappearances. Craig, under duress, leads Fletcher to the civilization. Craig, now obsessed with his power, proceeds to trample parts of their civilization, justifying his action as a means to demonstrate authority so that the little people will not behave poorly. Fletcher, in despair at the horror, apologizes to the little people.

In the final scene of the episode, Fletcher has fixed the ship and is ready to depart. When going to retrieve Craig, Fletcher finds a statue of Craig that the aliens were coerced into building. Fletcher, simply wanting to go back home and leaving the aliens in peace, begs Craig to return to the ship. Craig, steadfast on maintaining his godly position, aims a gun at Fletcher and convinces the captain to return to earth alone. Fletcher leaves Craig in his maddened state.

While Craig speaks to the little people of his plans for the future, a stomping sound accompanied by a mysterious shadow engulf the surrounding area. Just after claiming to protect the little people as their god, Craig is crushed by a giant foot. The frame scans upward to reveal that two giant aliens have arrived on the planet and have accidentally killed Craig. The giant alien picks Craig off his shoe and proceeds without concern for the dead earthling.

Chaim 1: Some conclude there is no God, there is no justice.

Chaim 2: Rabbi Yannai taught: There aren't always answers as to why some of the wicked prosper.

Chaim 1: Craig prospered?

Chaim 2: Right before he was stepped on.

Chaim 3: There's no justice when Craig hid God. He built his own babel. Torah 101: you're not God. We're here to create better worlds, not possess them.

Chaim 1: He should have read Job. He created a new life with Mrs. Job—after losing their ten children. Job and Mrs. Job's grief had to be never ending, but so was their opportunity to keep creating.

Chaim 3: Grief and distress can easily take us hostage.

Chaim 2: Not in discussion. Craig abandoned it by claiming to be God. When doctors of the Talmud prescribe that discussion should never cease, they mean no one gets to be God of the discussion.

Chaim 3: Discussion makes us tall. Craig was small with an unguarded tongue.

Chaim 1: What about Fletcher?

Chaim 2: He is Abel to Craig's Cain.

Chaim 3: A descendent of Balaam; grudging, arrogant, and proud.

Chaim 1: Goodness ran from him.

Chaim 3: It runs from those seeking power for themselves and who long for fame.

Chaim 2: Real discussion disrupts the will to power.

Chaim 3: What is real discussion?

Chaim 1: When the end of the discussion isn't known at the beginning of it. Could you imagine knowing the end of your child's life at their birth?

Chaim 2: No, but I also can't imagine where, how, and why I was conceived.

Chaim 3: What is wrong with you?! Does Chava let you eat like this?

Chaim 2: No.

Chaim 3: Pretend she's here. [Wiping Chaim 2's popcorn projectiles from his face]

Chaim 3: Things don't always make sense to us, but as Rabbi Yannai teaches: an explanation may not make sense, but this does not mean "sense" doesn't exist.

Chaim 2: This needs more salt. [Stands up to get salt for popcorn]

Chaim 3: Chava says no salt for you.

Chaim 2: Don't gossip about Chava. [Goes to get salt]

Chaim 3: The midrash here teaches to not seek power for yourself nor long for fame as did Craig. Do not crave the table of kings. Such cravings absent your obligations for the Other which makes one lonely.

Chaim 1: Hope is sometimes lost for the lonely.

Chaim 2: One has few, if any, to learn from when isolated.

Chaim 1: Is there dignity when isolated from others?

Chaim 2: If the other is Craig, there's plenty of dignity in isolation.

Chaim 3: The other side of this is that taught by the ethics of our parents: one who learns from someone else must treat that someone with respect.

THE GIFT

First broadcast on April 27, 1962, as the thirty-second episode of the third season, the midrash "The Gift" opens with news being brought into a small Mexican village concerning a UFO that crashed into the mountains. When the police went to investigate, the alien was claimed to have killed an officer named Salvador and wounded another. However, the officer (Paul Mazursky) bearing the news does say that he shot the alien twice.

The next scene shows a bartender, Manolo (Cliff Osmond), complaining of his guardianship over a boy named Pedro (Edmund Vargas), an orphan who cleans the bar, but is largely considered a weird child for his frequent absences at school and fascination with the night sky. A mysterious man by the name of Mr. Williams (Geoffrey Horne) soon enters the bar.

The bartender, paying little attention, asks the man to leave as it is too late to be serving drinks. However, the bartender soon realizes that Mr. Williams is the alien from the news. When the bartender goes to tell the authorities of the alien's location, Mr. Williams tackles the bartender, explaining that his actions were out of self-defense. Despite trying to explain that his intentions were peaceful, the cops proceeded with violent actions. A doctor in the bar provides assistance to Mr. Williams by performing an emergency surgery to remove the bullets lodged inside Mr. Williams from the police altercation. After the surgery, Mr. Williams gives a gift to Pedro.

During the surgery, Manolo finds a way to tell the army about the alien's whereabouts. Knowing this, Mr. Williams attempts to run for his ship by escaping out the back window. However, the army and local authorities find and corner him. Williams reiterates his claim that the death of the policeman at the mountains was an accident and encourages Pedro to show the authorities the gift. Out of fear for what is contained in the package, the police burn the gift. Mr. Williams then reaches out for Pedro, but the authorities, fearing that this was an act of violence, shoot and kill Mr. Williams. The doctor then picks up the burning gift, the remains of which are a card claiming that the aliens want to form a bond with earth and as a peace offering have provided the formula for a vaccine against all types of cancer.

Chaim 1: Again, we face a nomadic stranger, albeit a good one. How do you prepare yourself for an unfamiliar interrupting stranger, say, a person from a different background, a houseless person one passes on the street, those living with a hardship you do not face, or new immigrants who come to stay? Each of these obligates one into different responses for the stranger.

Chaim 3: Serling is obsessed with the nomadic stranger, the stranger who may take us from others, the silencer of discussion must be resisted, a necessary root of Serling's prophecy for democracy.

Chaim 2: Again, they assume they know the answer to: "Who are you?"

Chaim 1: Willful ignorance doesn't know how to ask that question.

Chaim 2: Such ignorance always staggers back to the underground—like a dying clown turning hearts into broken cups.

Chaim 3: This is why Serling instructs us to see ourselves in the chaos we make by our willful ignorance, . . . triggering our tongue but not our ears. One doesn't look for monsters outside the world to understand why Hitlers and Stalins succeed at home. Look in the mirror.

Chaim 1: "As Hillel declared: If I am not for myself, who will be for me? Only the person themselves has the power to correct [their] past mistakes—through proper repentance and a firm resolve to live by the laws of proper speech."[1]

Chaim 2: Hospitality means listening.

Chaim 3: "By exercising verbal restraint, one is saved from many sins."[2] I'm parched. Any Schnaaps?

Chaim 2: Before one creates worlds, one has heard the other's answer to "who are you?"

Chaim 3: Thirsty.

Chaim 1: Rabbi Kagan teaches from Talmud: "One should forever arouse [their] good inclination to subdue [their] bad inclination. Life is an ongoing struggle with one's evil inclination. One must forever be poised for battle and never be discouraged by failure. With knowledge of what the Torah requires of us and proper resolve, our efforts will ultimately succeed."[3]

Chaim 3: "By exercising verbal restraint, one is saved from many sins."[4]

---

1. Kagan, *Chofetz Chaim*, 371.
2. Kagan, *Chofetz Chaim*, 227.
3. Kagan, *Chofetz Chaim*, 63.
4. Kagan, *Chofetz Chaim*, 227.

Chaim 2: However, Rabbi Mattiah says: "Take the first step: greet others. It is an act of risk, of humility, since you may be ignored or put down. So be it: still greet the other party first, make the connection, break the barrier."[5]

TO SERVE MAN

The fifth midrash illuminates nomadic alien encounters with an intent to take over our world. It is from season 3, episode twenty-four, "To Serve Man," first broadcast on March 2, 1962. In it, Michael Chambers (Lloyd Bochner) recounts when the Kanamits (Richard Kiel), a nine-foot-tall telepathic alien species, first arrived on earth. Although the arrival of a UFO instigated a reaction of fear, tensions seem to ease after the Kanamits meet with the United Nations. The United Nations opens the floor to the Kanamits, not with any hostility, but certainly with some pensiveness. Exercising a great amount of decorum, the members of the United Nation question the purpose and intentions of the Kanamits. Naturally, there is some suspicion among the UN members, but they offer these speculations through a lens of logic rather than fear of danger. In doing so, the Kanamits are given the benefit of the doubt, which largely fits within the framework of welcoming the stranger.

The Kanamits explain that they seek only to use their advanced technology to establish peace on earth by offering resources such as chemicals that will enhance the fertility of land and force fields that will reduce the fear of war. The humans accept the offer and harmony is created among the nations of the world. People even begin to take vacations to the Kanamit world.

Despite the plentiful benefits brought by the Kanamits, the humans continue investigations on the Kanamits by preforming lie detector tests and decoding a book one of the Kanamits left at the UN meeting. However, Chambers explains in his narration that these actions were done out of custom more so than genuine mistrust.

The humans have grown to like the Kanamits and after the cryptography group discovers the title of the book is *To Serve Man*, any doubts concerning the Kanamits are assuaged . . . until the last moment of the episode. While Chambers boards a Kanamit ship to take a trip to their home planet, his partner Patty (Susan Cummings) arrives at the docking station, revealing that the book *To Serve Man* is not a book on how to better the

---

5. Neusner, *Torah from Our Sages*, 141.

life of man, but rather how to *cook* a man. Chambers fails to escape as the boarding ramp closes up.

Chaim 3: There were no Frisbees in the ovens. They threw Chambers right into it as the Nazis threw Europe into Hitler's willing executioners. No sunflowers are found on the mass graves of those obliterated. Chambers will burn in the Kanamit fires.

Chaim 1: Kanamits teach us to master our murderous drives just as the Bible teaches us to be nothing like the nomadic founder of the first city, Cain.

Chaim 2: We must guard our tongues from speaking Kanamit.

Chaim 3: People want a daddy to fix everything; when people follow someone trumpeting that they alone will fix everything, creativity and community die.

Chaim 2: Discussion can resist monolithic hate.

Chaim 1: Kanamits don't allow discussion.

Chaim 3: Chambers gave them the power to silence it.

Chaim 1: I don't trust anyone claiming they have the solution for us—as if it's a redux of the garden of Eden. Don't assume this stranger is a stranger you know. Can't dance with the devil.

Chaim 3: Chaim Rumkowski comes to mind.

Chaim 2: None of that. No gossip, not today.

Chaim 3: Seriously? He did what he did for the world to see. A Jew who thought he had an "in" with Nazis.

Chaim 2: We're here to talk about us, not him.

Chaim 3: We'll be him if we're not vigilant for others. That's Serling's directive. Hospitality isn't assuming you know, it's listening. How did Rebecca know a messenger approached? She studied him as he approached just as Moses studied a burning bush unconsumed by flames. I'd have run. Who stands and studies it? Moses. Serling is showing we will be burned, served to the world if we don't listen or watch. Rebecca and Moses both show listening is hospitality and they both heard and became more than they'd be if they clogged their ears with their own thoughts.

Chaim 2: True. It's not hospitable to assume you know the other.

Chaim 1: Seriously. Knowledge allows for little surprise. Listening yearns for it.

Chaim 3: Listening readies you for that which you're never ready.

Chaim 1: Serling demands we listen to the nomadic stranger. Be hospitable, but not a fool.

Chaim 2: A school "is not measured by how many good or bad students are in it, but by what the students consider good or bad."[6]

Chaim 3: As Rabbi Yannai says, "We do not have [an explanation] either for the prosperity of the wicked or for the suffering of the righteous."[7]

Chaim 1: To resist being owned before one is served up dead is Serling's prophecy.

Chaim 2: I have to go!

Chaim 1: Where?

Chaim 2: Home. I need to bathe Sam, Israel, David, Shmuel, and Yitzhak.

Chaim 1: You couldn't have done this before you came?

Chaim 3: What's Chava doing?

Chaim 2: Bathing Sarah, Rebecca, Leah, Rachel, and Naomi. Chava wants the bowl back. I'm taking the popcorn.

Chaim 3: Ask her if they can skip a day.

Chaim 2: They can't.

Chaim 3: They study so hard, they smell? Text her and ask. [Chaim 2 texts her]

Chaim 2: She'll do it. Our study is creating the world, she says.

Chaim 3: Can she talk to my wife?

Chaim 2: I learned long ago to never question my sister, Eve.

Chaim 3: At least Eve salts popcorn.

Chaim 1: Eve's popcorn could use some butter.

Chaim 3: Not when you're around. You get it on your fingers and then all over our fabrics.

---

6. Zeitchik, *Sparks of Mussar*, 148.
7. Neusner, *Torah from Our Sages*, 141.

PROBE 7: OVER AND OUT

The ninth episode of the fifth season aired on November 29, 1963, and opens on a pilot named Colonel Cook (Richard Basehart), who finds himself in a dire situation: he has crashed his spacecraft Probe 7 into a foreign planet about 4.3 light years from his home. The ship is in an unusable condition with frayed wires, minimal functioning electronic equipment, and zero fuel. Colonel Cook is not in much better shape than the ship, having broken his arm in the landing.

As calm as one could be in such circumstances, Cook calls home base to explain his circumstances. In response to Cook's request for a rescue ship, the general, named Larrabee, explains that no rescue ship could reach such a far distance and that Cook would just have to make the repairs.

After receiving such devastating news, Cook emerges from the ship to find that the world is rich in vegetation, but severely lacking in sentient life. In his second transmission with base, Cook states that the world could be inhabitable due to having a gravitational pull and atmospheric pressure similar to his home world. Nevertheless, Cook wants to return home and once again asks for a rescue team to be sent. Unfortunately for Cook, rumors of an imminent war have been stirring on his planet and Larrabee (Harold Gould), recognizing the needs of the many are greater than the needs of the individual, cannot justify helping the isolated pilot. The news proves even grimmer the next day, when Larrabee declares that war has officially broken out and that the space team will be relocating due to nearby bombings. Recognizing the hopelessness of the situation, Cook asks if there is any reason to make future transmissions, to which Larrabee responds, "Yes, Colonel, two points: one, to help your loneliness, and two, to see if your own world exists."

That night, no longer anticipating a return home, Cook emerges from the ship and discovers circles etched in the dirt. Taking this as a sign of life, Cook joyously announces his presence and tries to coax out his new companion. Cook's shouts of joy are abruptly silenced as a thrown rock hits him on the side of the head and knocks him out.

In the morning, Cook awakens with his face in pain and heads back to the ship. Just when Cook thinks he has finally found peace, the back room of the ship is suddenly closed and locked shut. Grabbing a piece of metal just in case of another attack, Cook tries to speak reasonably to the enigmatic figure to get them to emerge. Realizing such an encroaching approach would prove futile, Cook exits the ship. This new plan proves successful, as Cook sees bushes rustling next to him. Seizing the opportunity to meet the elusive figure, Cook chases after the rustling and aggressively grabs at a leg . . . only to look up and see that this leg is attached to a woman (Antoinette Bower). With his heart now softened by the fairer sex, Cook throws down his metal rod and tries to communicate with her. Cook finds that the two do not share a common language, which he remedies by drawing diagrams in the ground to explain how he ended up on the planet. The woman, named Norda, explains she crashed after fleeing her own planet because it had spun out of orbit. Believing he has made peace, Cook gets up to look for food with Norda and grabs the metal rod. Norda, still with some trepidation, understands this as an act of aggression and runs away.

In the final scene, Cook opens the door of his ship to find Norda standing outside. Diplomatically, Cook explains that he has found an area rich in vegetation where he intends to live and invites Norda to join him. Claiming that he will need to learn to verbally communicate with his companion, Cook picks up a pile of dirt and asks Norda what she calls the substance in her language. Norda claims that she calls dirt "Erd-thah." Smoothing out the foreign word for dirt, Cook says that the planet will be called "Earth." With their new home now given a name, Cook tries to explain his own name again, saying, "Cook. Cook. Adam Cook. Adam Cook." To this, Norda responds with her full name, "Norda. Eve." Happily, Cook claims he shall call his new companion Eve. The episode ends with Adam Cook and Eve Norda in a garden-like area in which Norda breaks an apple off a tree and implores Cook to eat the food.

Chaim 1: As scripture says, we are children. As tradition reads, we are builders.

Chaim 2: Let's go.

Chaim 3: I don't plow.

Chaim 2: Creating is hard work.

Chaim 1: It is necessary to work hard at climbing the levels of ethics . . . just as a mountain climber must strain to climb a mountain.[8]

Chaim 3: Who do you know that climbs mountains?

Chaim 1: You. You climbed out of the destruction of Jewry.

Chaim 3: As Primo Levi said, liars and thieves survived as the angels died.

---

8. Zeitchik, *Sparks of Mussar*, 22.

Chaim 1: "It is impossible to win the battle against the evil inclination."[9] But you do every day. I see it when you study Torah.

Chaim 2: Every day you fortify your heart against your evil inclination.

Chaim 3: Let us not forget the wicked live long lives, getting paid for bad deeds.

Chaim 2: We are to create ways out.

Chaim 1. The opportunity never leaves. That's what this last midrash shows. With a good heart—even in the midst of cowboy colonialism picking fruit from trees one ought to leave alone—one has the creative opportunity to build new worlds out of tradition. We begin again as directed in this midrash's reference to Adam and Eve. Just when all seemed lost, hope is realized in speaking a new direction.

Chaim 3: Do not expect me to plow.

Chaim 2: You can milk cows.

Chaim 3: You saw a cow on that planet?

Chaim 1: In time with Hashem's direction.[10]

Chaim 2: "As soon as a good thought came to mind, R'Yisroel Meir immediately set about carrying it out."[11]

Chaim 1: The more Rabbi Meir did, the more he ran from honor.

Chaim 3: Honor can embolden one in bad ways.

[Haayim enters the room.]

Haayim: There's no one on that planet to honor them. I—I brought rugelach and schnaaps to dishonor you all. [They laugh.]

Chaim 1: Glad you're back.

Chaim 2: So soon?

Hayim: The pastors also play at night.

[The camera pulls back from the three rabbis sitting in what looks like an ordinary Yeshiva to reveal a window full of Martian faces observing them intently. Above them is a sign, "Earth Rabbis in Their Natural Setting."]

---

9. Zeitchik, *Sparks of Mussar*, 22.

10. Hashem is a Hebrew name of God. It means "The Name," i.e., the unnameable Name.

11. Zeitchik, *Sparks of Mussar*, 219.

Rod Serling: Three rabbis named Chaim reflect on lessons from a television program that was not mere entertainment, but like midrash, instructed us to resist fascism, waking the viewer into communal action against threats to it, showing the viewer who to be and how to act. Responding not only to Nazi horror, but also to nomadic politicians stealing our community by claiming to be our savior, like the period's Senator Joseph McCarthy. The rabbis' discourse reveals that this is not a fight one wins and then life beautifully goes on, rather, this is a fight we fight every day until we die. Community is both created and fought for. If not, we lose it, as Adam and Eve lost Eden and as David almost lost Israel by imposing his will when he raped BatSheba and murdered her husband. Instead, we should resist selfication and listen to the Other. A lesson they learned not only in the Torah and Talmud, but also in . . . The Twilight Zone.

Chapter 7

Seeing Is *Not* Believing

The Twilight Zone, Candid Camera, and *Mission: Impossible*

THE BOOK HAS FOCUSED on the life of Rod Serling in order to locate his Jewishness in *The Twilight Zone* when viewed on its own. In this chapter, we adopt a different stance in which we will pull the camera back historically and see *The Twilight Zone* as part of a larger movement in television programming of the early TV period. That movement included shows that were written by, produced by, and starred Jews and can therefore be interpreted through a social-historical Jewish lens that is shaped by both the Jewish American experience of the time and the global-historical-political events of the time and the era immediately preceding.

When we take such a look, we find a curious collection of three programs that one might not think of as connected at first glance: *The Twilight Zone, Candid Camera,* and *Mission: Impossible*. These programs come from different genres and appealed to different audiences, yet they have one central, indeed on might argue essential, element in common. All of these shows employed as a functional plot element the idea that the world was not as it seemed. This may appear *prima facie* to be a thin thread with which to sew them together, but the denial of a radical empiricism turns out to be historically significant from a Jewish perspective, especially in the decades following the end of World War II.

SEEING IS BELIEVING: EMPIRICISM, MODERNITY, AND JEWISH EMANCIPATION

Within the Jewish intellectual tradition, there has always been tension between the mystics and the philosophers, between those who believe knowledge, insight, and wisdom are disclosed through mysterious Divine sources accessible only to those whose minds are properly disposed to turn away from the world and others who think it derives from the use of human reason when applied both to sacred writings and to the contexts within the world.

The Judaic religion originated as a temple-worship cult in the Middle East. The Kohanim and the Levites were privileged members of the early community. Serving as priests at the Temple, they alone possessed access to the Divine. Collecting the traditional stories that had been passed down orally, they constructed the canonical texts that functioned as narrative histories, as moral parables, and as a social contract for one of the first agricultural communities.

When the Jews were driven away from their ancestral lands at various times by the Assyrians, the Babylonians, and the Greeks, the group still needed to practice its rituals. As the practices were Temple-based, this was a problem. They could not take the Temple with them into exile, but they could take the book. As such, when forced away from their land—*ha'aretz*—the text took on a central importance it did not have during the periods where the Jews had access to their Temple.

While this text, like all texts, requires interpretation to elicit meaning, the question became more critical in exile. The Torah and associated books began as a social contract for an agrarian society that clearly spoke about the need to avoid cities (see the stories of Sodom and Gomorrah). But when the Jews had to flee their land, they generally ended up in cities. Taking this document that emerged from a pastoral context into an urban setting for which it was not designed required wrestling with how to re-understand the laws, the mitzvot, in this radically different situation. Textual interpretation thereby became central.

Sophistication in textual interpretation has nothing to do with being born in a particular caste. Talented scholars can come from anywhere and the focus on the Book instead of the Temple changed the religious power dynamic within the religious portion of the community. So, when the Jews returned and rebuilt the Temple for the final time in the classical world, a division arose. On the one side, the Sadducees kept the old way of privileging the Temple, the priests, and the mystical element. On the other, the Pharisees elevated the Book, the interpreters, and the intellectual. The Romans (at first), left the internal power structure alone as long as taxes were paid. The Sadducees saw this as positive continuity, home rule. The Pharisees, on the other hand, saw it as capitulation, as collusion with the colonizers. The fault line deepened.

Ultimately, a change in Roman policy and increasing anti-occupation political action led to the final expulsion of the Jews from the Holy Land in the classical era giving rise to the diaspora that led to far-flung Jewish minority communities locating themselves across the globe. The diaspora settled the Sadducee/Pharisee debate for good and Jews became "people of the Book," with the interpretive approach becoming centrally embedded in the religion. The priests with direct access to the Divine were replaced with rabbis, wise scholars who mined the text for insight and wisdom.

The means of discovering truth in the text, however, became another point of contention. Some rabbis, such as Maimonides in twelfth-century Spain, contended that text-based rational argumentation was the route by which humans could come to understand the meaning of the Torah. Maimonides was not only among the greatest biblical scholars in history but also a philosopher in the Aristotelian tradition and renowned as the greatest doctor of his time.[1] He used a scientific approach to medicine and was so famous for his skills that it is purported that, during the Crusades, King Richard the Lionheart asked Maimonides to be his court physician.[2] As a philosopher and a scientist, Maimonides had a rational/empirical approach to knowledge.

But other rabbis disagreed with this path. Mystics, who launched the Kabbalistic school, contended that rational thought was far too blunt an instrument. It would never be capable of digging deeply enough into the text to uncover the deeply hidden truths woven into and buried deep within it. Rabbi Moses de Leon at the same time and roughly same place, wrote in his book *Mishkan Ha-Eduth*:

> [T]here are hidden mysteries and secret things which are unknown to men. You will now see that I am revealing deep and secret mysteries which the holy sages regarded as sacred and hidden, profound matters which properly speaking are not fit for revelation so they may not be made a target for the wit of every

---

1. Heschel, *Maimonides*.
2. Steinschneider, "An Introduction to the Arabic Literature of the Jews," 105.

idle person. These holy men of old have pondered all their lives over these things and have hidden them, and did not reveal them to everyone, now I have come to reveal them.[3]

The idea is that there is shallow and deep knowledge. Maimonides' rational philosophical approach, these mystics contends, only gets you to the shallow knowledge. Deep knowledge requires something other than reason, something only spiritually accessible.

So, there has long been a fault line in the Jewish community between those, on the one hand, who contended that reason is the key to insight and wisdom, and those, on the other hand, who saw mystical means as the key. The philosophical side ascended in the eighteenth and nineteenth century with the Haskalah, the Jewish Enlightenment. Like the non-Jewish European Enlightenment, it was a reaction to (not against) the scientific revolution. René Descartes, the seventeenth-century French philosopher, held that "the other sciences . . . borrow their principles from philosophy."[4] But, the fact is, philosophy is a reactive discipline. It was the scientific work of the likes of Descartes, Copernicus, Leibniz, and Newton that made the Enlightenment necessary.

With a new understanding of the motion of the planets, the old Aristotelean worldview became untenable. As the official doctrine of the Catholic Church drew from Aristotelianism, each new advance in science that took us beyond Aristotle's theories undermined the Church's claim to infallibility and thereby its influence. This suited the Protestants just fine and they pushed forward scientific study with a clear political agenda. The monarchies of Europe owed their stable power to the doctrine of the Divine right of kings, which was itself underwritten by the unquestionable authority of the Catholic Church. The Protestant opposition to theological hierarchy led to a distaste for political hierarchy and the idea of a personal relationship with God coupled easily with an embrace of democratic norms. The rise of science—an epistemological endeavor in which all observers possess equal access to worldly truth—fitted hand-in-glove with the Protestant view that all of God's children have equal access to God's ear and God's word. The Church was no longer needed to mediate the relationship through its hierarchical structure, and as such the Reformation led to some groups championing political structures that tore down the old hierarchies of fixed power

---

3. Quoted in Scholem, *Major Trends in Jewish Mysticism*, 201.
4. Descartes, *Discourse on Method*, 5.

and redistributing that power to all. It is in this way that science, religion, and politics became intertwined in the wake of the scientific revolution.[5]

We are all created in God's image, the Enlightenment thinkers contended, so we all share in the essential human elements. Chief among these is rationality. A perfect God could only create a perfect world.[6] The world's perfection must imply a fully rational construction and the human mind would be God's instrument for its appreciation. Since all humans are created in the Divine image, all humans possess rationality.

Hence, the Protestants start from a place of universality, of equality among all people with the possession of the intellectual capacity to find truth. This is consistent with the intellectual basis of democratic rule. Deliberative democracy allows competing options to be pitted against each other with the citizen making a rational choice for the one most likely to be the best.

Contrast this with the Catholic approach to knowledge. Humans are not inherently equal, each with the same access to truth. The pope, when speaking about matters of doctrine, is infallible because he and he alone has direct access to God. That knowledge then passes through a mediating hierarchy of cardinals, archbishops, bishops, priests, and finally the laity. That sense of epistemological inequality was consistent with monarchy, especially given the doctrine of the divine right of kings.

Hence, it is not accidental that we saw the rise of Protestantism, science, and democracy at the same time. Religion, science, and politics were deeply intertwined. Advocates of democracy, largely Protestants who had democratized revealed and then natural truth, thus were led to assert equal political rights for all.

But the Catholics and the Protestants were not the only humans there. The Jews of the time who engaged in this conversation waved their hands wildly over their heads and jumped up and down shouting that Jews, too, are humans and therefore created in the image of God and thereby are rational and so should also have equal political rights. Realizing this made many of the Protestants in the Enlightenment uneasy. They didn't really mean *all* humans, just *us* humans. To which the Jews responded, "No . . . you clearly said *all* humans." Enlightenment modernism with its commitment to science and democracy held within it the seeds of emancipation for oppressed Jews throughout Europe.

5. Merton, "Science, Technology and Society in Seventeenth Century England."
6. Leibniz, "Fifth Correspondence with Clarke," 252.

As a result, thinkers of the Haskalah from Moses Mendelssohn to Isaac Abraham Euchel worked to reformulate Judaism in a way that would update it, allow it the flexibility to embrace science, and open it to secular moral and political values. Doing so freed Jews from the anti-Semitic restrictions that disallowed the conditions for a flourishing human life. Modernism was the key to acceptance, to tearing down the walls of bigotry that kept them trapped in their insular villages, and thereby opened the world up to them.[7]

Of course, there were those for whom those walls were self-reinforced. Traditionalist, later Orthodox rabbis, chafed at the modernist turn. Rabbi Moishe Sofer proclaimed unambiguously, "The new is forbidden by the Torah."[8] Jews lived among Jews not because the gentile world was keeping them out, but rather because they needed to stay together to protect Judaism and the Jewish way of life, which was threatened by the romanticized modernism.

But the appeal of modernism, with all of the benefits it conveyed, was intoxicating. The *goyische* Europeans never made fully good on the promised equality of their Enlightenment principles, but the new orientation offered Jews a bright future.

When we move into the twentieth century, modernist Jews can be found challenging orthodoxy in virtually all fields of the arts, sciences, and letters. Jews led the way in atonal music, Dadaist art, and modernist architecture.[9] Jews were making up a major part of the avant-garde in intellectual endeavors across the spectrum. But nowhere was the success more notable than in the sciences. Jews were being appointed to prestigious professorships for the first time. Despite being a miniscule proportion of the population, Jews won Nobel Prizes at a staggering rate.[10]

Science is the art of taking what you see and using it to infer what is real. Modernism begins with the presumption of a rational universe, that is, a well-ordered universe whose governing principles are accessible to the human mind. If the mind is properly tuned with the rules of reasoning and careful observations are made, then we can learn the underlying guiding rules from what we observe. Science, to the modernist mind, achieves the goal of Isaac Newton—reading the mind of God. In embracing this

---

7. Feiner, *Haskalah and History*.
8. Katz, *A House Divided*, 62.
9. Gay, *Freud, Jews, and Other Germans*.
10. Efron, *A Chosen Calling*.

scientific modernism, Jews ensconced themselves thoroughly in the new worldview and the emerging new world order.

Perhaps the epitome of the modernist Jew, certainly the most famous, is Albert Einstein. Einstein's special and general theories of relativity are full of strange and counter-intuitive results. Objects shrink in the direction of motion. Moving clocks run slower the faster they move. Nothing can exceed the speed of light. Spacetime bends according to density of mass and energy within it. As bizarre as this all seems, the reason we believe it is that the observations we make conform to its predictions. During eclipses, stars in the vicinity of the sun appear out of place due to the bending of light. The orbit of Mercury is not a simple ellipse, but an intricate daisy-like pattern perfectly predicted by the Einstein Field Equations.[11] Our minds may boggle at all of this, but as the Nobel Prize-winning results of the LIGO measurements of gravitational waves[12] show us, it is in fact the way the world seems to work.

In the end, then, it is the old adage "seeing is believing" that sits beneath the greatest advance of the modernist mind. Empiricism, that is, a commitment to making sense of the world based upon observation, was the key to Jewish emancipation and advancement from the times of Maimonides through the age of Einstein.

SEEING IS NOT BELIEVING: GERMANY AND THE DEATH OF EMANCIPATORY EMPIRICISM

In the winter of 1933, Einstein was in residency as a visitor at the California Institute of Technology in Pasadena. It was there that he learned of the election of Adolf Hitler as chancellor of Germany. (Never forget that Hitler was elected.) At that moment, he knew he could never return to the land of his birth.[13]

He had left Germany as a high school student, fleeing to Italy to be with his family who had previously moved there. Also, he left to avoid the mandatory military service.[14] He ended up in Switzerland, where he finished high school, college, became a patent clerk, and after a brief stint teaching in Prague, returned to Switzerland to work as a professor. It was

11. Gimbel, *Einstein*.
12. Overbye, "Gravitational Waves Detected."
13. Clark, *Einstein*, 550–57.
14. Clark, *Einstein*, 36.

the country he loved the most, keeping his Swiss passport out of adoration of the culture, the pacifism, and the cosmopolitanism. As a teenager, he had surrendered his German passport and was determined never to return to the country of his birth.

But one of his heroes, Max Planck, made him an offer he could not refuse and lured him to Berlin.[15] Life in Germany was cultured. Colleagues were collegial. Like so many other German Jews, things seemed good . . . and seeing is believing . . . or so they thought.

When World War I began, Einstein was horrified by the violence of the war and the barbarity shown by the German military in, for example, the so-called rape of Belgium in which war crimes were brutally committed against civilians. He was also gobsmacked by the response from those he respected. In response to German atrocities, many intellectuals bought into a "two Germanys" hypothesis wherein there were Germans connected with the military who supported the violence, but then there was a separate Germany that was the source of the art, science, industry, and culture that the rest of the world looked at with awe and respect. The German intellectuals and industrialists whom the outside world adored surely were not supporting the brutality.

Then the *Manifesto of the 93* was published, wherein those very figures added their signature to a letter that explicitly sought to deflate the "Two Germanys." Here were the most notable members of this "other" Germany publicly asserting for all to read that German militarism, German nationalism, and German culture are all one and the same. The people he thought he knew were not the people he thought he knew.[16]

This was a common occurrence for Jews who had warm relations with their delightful neighbors . . . until they suddenly didn't. The world turned upside down with such a dizzying speed that the mind could not comprehend how people who had been friends now viewed them as vicious enemies. Had they been wrong all along about the friendships or had things changed so quickly? The world no longer made sense.

Jews had been emancipated politically because of a philosophical commitment to Enlightenment values that elevated the scientific, and science relied on inductive inferences based on repeated observation. Find patterns in how you see the world and then generalize them to laws of nature. Jews had become good at this and some had become doctors and scientists of

---

15. Clark, *Einstein*, 212.
16. Clark, *Einstein*, 228.

great renown. These positions garnered social capital and slowly the anti-Semitic political barriers were receding, creating a positive feedback loop that furthered the commitment to empiricism. Inductively, this pattern should have continued.

But it didn't. After the German loss in World War I, things got worse. And then they became unspeakable. It would have been one thing if those who carried out the genocidal atrocities had been monsters all along. But, by in large, they hadn't. These were normal people, neighbors and acquaintances, people they thought they knew. Those people joined in. Those people became a part of it. It betrayed the eyes and betrayed the mind. It is commonly said that "the road to hell is paved with good intentions." This may be true, but it is also the case that the road to Auschwitz was paved with empirically supported inductive inferences concerning the character and friendship of neighbors. Jews wondered if they could ever trust their eyes and ears again.

THE TWILIGHT ZONE AND THE THREAT OF EMPIRICAL EQUIVALENCE

Serling contested whether eyes and ears were trustworthy. On the one hand, there were episodes of the show that demonstrated a commitment to empiricism. Consider the episode "Nightmare at 20,000 Feet," first broadcast on October 11, 1963, and written by Richard Matheson, in which salesman Bob Wilson (William Shatner), returning home on a flight after time in a sanitorium due to a nervous breakdown, sees a gremlin tampering with the electronics of the plane's engines beneath a plate on the wing it has pried up mid-flight. The gremlin allows itself to be seen by Wilson, but hides whenever anyone else is watching. At the end of the episode, when Wilson has stolen an officer's gun and shot the gremlin thereby saving the flight, he is thought by everyone else to have suffered another nervous breakdown in which he was trying to commit suicide. But in the final shot of the episode, the tampered with plate covering the electronics is shown. In his outro, Serling says,

> The flight of Mr. Robert Wilson has ended now, a flight not only from point A to point B, but also from the fear of recurring mental breakdown. Mr. Wilson has that fear no longer . . . though, for the moment, he is, as he has said, alone in this assurance. Happily, his conviction will not remain isolated too much longer, for happily,

tangible manifestation is very often left as evidence of trespass, even from so intangible a quarter as the Twilight Zone.

Notice that it is explicitly stated that a "tangible manifestation" is considered to be "evidence." In other words, seeing is believing. Empiricism is accepted.

Of course, the functional plot device within the episode is that only Wilson sees what Wilson sees. No one else sees it. But because of the previous nervous breakdown there are two different interpretations of what Wilson saw that are both consistent with experience. Either Wilson is having delusions from mental problems or he is seeing what he is seeing. Both are consistent with the observations giving rise to what philosophers call "empirical equivalence."

Two distinct realities are empirically equivalent when they are different from each other, yet convey to an observer the same complete set of sense perceptions, that is, if they are different, but you could never tell by looking. Gottfried Leibniz postulated his "Principle of the Identity of Indiscernibles,"[17] arguing that if two things shared all observational properties, then they are, in fact, identical, that is, are the same exact thing. This demands complete in-principle discernibility. The notion of empirical equivalence used here is different from Leibnizian indiscernibility in that we are limiting ourselves to a single observer. It is the sort of Cartesian evil demon/brain-in-a-vat/*The Matrix*/*Truman Show*-type indiscernibility where there is a difference between the world as perceived and the world as it is, but, for a given individual, there is no way to tell the difference.

It is the sort of empirical equivalence experienced by the Jews of Europe before World War II. It is also the same sort that will be the central operative elements in three television series: *The Twilight Zone*, *Candid Camera*, and *Mission: Impossible*. In the case of *The Twilight Zone*, it will be one recurring theme that functions as the basis for disorienting horror.

Indeed, we can take the very first episode in the history of the series as a prime example. Episode 1 of season 1 of *The Twilight Zone* is entitled "Where Is Everybody?" which was written by Rod Serling and aired on October 2, 1959. The episode opens with Mike Ferris, played by Earl Holliman, finding himself in the small town of Oakwood, but not sure who he is or how he got there. He wanders into a diner to find it abandoned, not dusty and long abandoned, but so recently abandoned that there are eggs

---

17. Leibniz, "Fifth Correspondence with Clarke," 62.

on the grill and coffee hot in the pot. He helps himself to breakfast and leaves money in the till.

He searches the town for anyone who can tell him anything about anything, but to no avail. The pay phone will not reach anyone. One shop seems to have people, but they turn out to be mannequins. Indeed, one is even in the passenger side of a car leading Ferris to wonder if some bizarre force had turned real people into mannequins. He is alone. The world is devoid of human life, but for him.

Yet traces of humanity repeatedly present themselves. Everywhere he goes, every place is empty but contains artifacts of normal life: eggs on the grill, shaving cream and a razor in the prison, movies being run, ice cream in the freezer case and fixings ready to be put on sundaes in the ice cream parlor which has a sign for the special of the day. It is as if humans were there and then vanished all together just moments before his arrival.

In a rack in the ice cream parlor are multiple copies of a book titled *The Last Man on Earth.* Was Ferris, in fact, the last man on earth? If so, why? What happened to everyone else? This was the era of the Cold War, was this the result of some new version of a hydrogen bomb that vaporized human life, but left the material world otherwise unchanged? This was the start of the space race with the Soviet Union and the heart of the UFO craze, did aliens abduct everyone? What happened? Ferris and the viewer both try to figure it out.

Ferris slowly but steadily finds himself losing his grip on his sanity. He eventually flies into a blind rage. The solitude leads to madness and as he approaches a crosswalk with a button on the pole of the traffic light to signal the need to cross, he urgently and repeatedly presses the button. It is an odd action. There are no cars. He could just cross the street in complete safety. Yet, he pushes it, crying out that he needs help.

The camera blurs out and then comes back into focus and there is Ferris in a small booth pushing a panic button. It turns out that Mike Ferris is, in fact, a member of the Air Force and is in training to be an astronaut. He is in a sensory deprivation booth, undergoing an experiment to see how people would fare in the emptiness and loneliness of space. When Ferris is brought back to consciousness, he is taken away on a stretcher. He tells his skeptical superiors that next time he will do better and asserts a "go-get-'em" attitude toward space travel.

What is important for this discussion is that we have a person who has clear and distinct observations of the world. He hears the music on the jukebox. He enjoys a hot fudge sundae. There is a unified, coherent set of observations of the world. From these observations, Ferris makes reasonable inferences about how the world is. But the world is not really that way. Despite all of the observational evidence he could collect, he would not know how the world really is. And, most importantly, this deception, this false picture of the world, is dangerous. To be deceived about reality is to be in peril, to perhaps lose one's identity as a person.

Indeed, it is technology (in this case, space exploration) that poses a threat to being human. In the closing monologue of the episode, Serling says,

> The barrier of loneliness: the palpable, desperate need of the human animal to be with his fellow man. Up there, up there in the vastness of space, in the void that is sky, up there is an enemy known as isolation. It sits there in the stars waiting, waiting with the patience of eons, forever waiting . . . in The Twilight Zone.

Space flight is—and at the time was held up as—the apex of the success of modernism. This was two years after the Russians launched Sputnik, the year after the Mercury project first began working to put an American in space, and the same year that NASA launched the Discoverer satellite and the Pioneer rocket for a lunar flyby. The idea of putting a man on the moon, which would become a reality within a decade, was in the air and was seen as the greatest conceivable achievement of humanity.

Until Copernicus, we had thought the earth the literal center of the universe. Until Darwin, we had considered ourselves unique in being made in the image of God. But then Copernicus made us just another planet in a seemingly limitless universe and Darwin made us just another animal. But here was humanity reasserting itself on the universe. We would not be conquered by space, instead the human spirit guided by the modernist credo would triumphantly assert humanity upon the cosmos itself. Space travel made us more than mere animals. It made us transcendent beings.

But not in the eyes of Serling. Serling's first episode of *The Twilight Zone* sends two warnings to those who would naively embrace the modernist enthusiasm. First, it has the capacity to lead to dehumanization. Space travel, modernism's greatest product, may, in the end, produce loneliness, alienation, keeping us from our most basic need of community, of connectedness, of intersubjectivity. As Primo Levi says of his time in a Nazi death camp, "A curious effect of this void, a need for communication, is the undernourished brain suffers from a particular hunger of its own."[18] If we trust the brain too much, we may lose that which is needed by the human heart.

Secondly, this modernist stance requires a thoroughgoing acceptance of "seeing is believing," that is, that the world is as it seems. It was this belief that initially led to Jewish emancipation in Europe with the values of the Enlightenment, but it was also this belief that allowed Jews in central Europe to be caught off guard with the rise of Nazism. Serling is a Jew who had learned not to trust the way things seemed and was now trying to teach that lesson to the broader American community. What Jews had learned because of Hitler in World War II, Serling was now trying to show to America as a whole in the new Cold War. Empirical equivalence is always a possibility and with it came the inability to realize invisible dangers that may be lurking beneath the appearances. Serling championed the Pharisaic/Maimonides/Einstein empiricist strain of Jewish thought in embracing the "sci" in "sci-fi," but coupled it with a Sadduceeic/Kabalistic mystical sensibility. We see that in this first episode of *The Twilight Zone* and the leitmotif of "things aren't how they seem" became one of the central plot mechanisms throughout the entire run of the series.

CANDID CAMERA AND THE JOY OF EMPIRICAL EQUIVALENCE

A second series that turns on the limited notion of empirical equivalence is *Candid Camera*. While it may seem odd, Allen Funt originally launched the idea on radio, the program beginning as *The Candid Microphone*, and was a forerunner of prank call comedy of the sort one can find today from Jim Florentine or on the Comedy Central program *Crank Yankers*, but its inspiration came from an insight Funt had while serving in the US Army during World War II.[19]

Like Rod Serling and so many other Jewish men, Funt served in the armed forces to oppose the hateful policies of Adolf Hitler. Unlike Serling, however, he did not volunteer, but was drafted into the service. The Army was both a natural and a strange place for someone like Funt. He came

---

18. Levi, *The Saved and the Drowned*, 81.
19. Simon, "The Changing Definition of Reality Television," 180.

from the rough streets of Brooklyn and was a streetwise tough guy and an accomplished amateur boxer. He knew how to fight.[20]

The ability to use his fists, however, would seem odd for someone with his later background, an Ivy League graduate with an art degree. Funt attended Cornell University, where he studied fine art. Realizing that his talent as a painter was insufficient to put food on the table, he entered the world of advertising and was primarily focused on radio clients.[21]

In the golden age of radio, programs had a single sponsor. Lipton Tea sponsored Arthur Godfrey's *Talent Scouts*. Canada Dry sponsored *The Guy Lombardo Show*. Unlike the commercial television sponsorship model in which networks developed and produced shows and then sought multiple sponsors to run short ads during the airing of the show, on radio, the sponsor bore the entire financial burden of development and production. It thereby also controlled everything from casting to content. As a result, the sponsor's product would be as much a part of the program as the stars.

Funt's advertising work was as an "idea man," that is, he worked with the writers of the radio programs his clients were sponsoring to develop new show concepts and ways to incorporate the product into the show. It was creative work that taught him the ropes when it came to media presentation. In the Army, he made use of this background when he was assigned to the Army Signal Corps, and was put to work producing radio shows for the Army to keep troops entertained in the field and to create fund-raising events for war bonds.

He used it to create two programs that would pave the way to *Candid Camera*. The first was called *Behind the Dog Tags: The Show That Makes G.I. Wishes Come True* and did exactly what the title says. Funt would ask soldiers for their wishes and look for the strangest of them, wishes like swimming in beer, and then would make the wish come true and tape the bizarre event. From this, Funt learned how to use spectacle, yet understate it in a way that keeps an audience.[22]

The second program was entitled *The Gripe Booth* in which GIs would register their complaints about Army life. People are at their most human when they are kvetching, so Funt encouraged normal people to complain about normal things, creating a bond between those on the air and in the audience. But Funt noticed something odd. When the soldiers knew the

---

20. Nadis, "Citizen Funt," 13.
21. Nadis, "Citizen Funt," 13.
22. Nadis, "Citizen Funt," 14.

mic was hot, when they saw the red light go on signaling that they were on the air, they would tighten up, sometimes freezing entirely. But if he could catch them candidly, just talking, their personality would come out and what they said would be more affective and certainly funnier.[23]

Funt combined these two insights after war on *Candid Microphone* which debuted in 1947. The next year, early in television's infancy, Funt changed media and moved the show to the small screen, changing its name to *Candid Camera*.[24] The show would be divided into several bits. Each bit would be comprised of an initial segment in which the context of the gag would be explained. The gag would center around a normal social context in which a random person would commonly find themselves. However, the show will have set up some element of the context to not function as one would expect. In one instance, for example, the spoons in a diner were made so that the heat from a standard cup of coffee would cause the head of the spoon to fall off the stem. In another, a car had its engine removed and then sent into a gas station.

Once the home viewers knew what to look for, a series of videos filmed by hidden cameras would be shown with special emphasis not on the gag itself, but on the person's reaction to something happening where they cannot believe their eyes. In the case of the dissolving spoon, we see a string of customers add sugar or cream to their cup of coffee and stare in shock when only half of their spoon emerges from stirring. In the case of the car without an engine, the driver (a woman) asks the attendant to check the oil, but when the gas station attendant gets under the hood, he is confronted with no engine. Yet, he just saw the car roll into the station. He had seen it driving.

In some cases, there is an explosive reaction where the person freaks out at reality not conforming to expectations. Other times, there is bafflement and double and triple takes. Sometimes, there is a person desperately trying to figure out what happened. And yet others who play it cool and try to act as if everything is normal.

Throughout the showing of the clips, Funt would speak before and over in a casual tone, as if we were in a room with him, often telling the audience what warranted special attention. "In this next one," Funt might say, "watch the man's eyes. He's going to realize what is happening and check to see if anyone else saw before he reacts." The calm, knowing tone of these

23. Nadis, "Citizen Funt," 17.
24. Simon, "The Changing Definition of Reality Television," 180.

tips lent an intimacy to the show. You got the sense that Funt was an old friend talking directly to you.

The bit ends when the videos switch from the meat of the gag to the end when Funt would come over to one of the people fooled, point to the hidden camera, and say the famous catchphrase, "Smile, you're on *Candid Camera.*" At that point, the person realizes they have been had, that the deviation from normal is all a gag, and the result is almost uniformly laughter at being able to see the larger picture. It may be a single reveal or a series, but those always ended the segment.

What is important about this segment is that we at home, the voyeurs getting joy from surveilling the "victim," get to see that the "victim" is not actually a victim because the reaction is one of relief and laughter. There is initially shock and then a joyful release that could range anywhere from a "you got me" smirk to a full-body guffaw at the prank. By seeing the person on the screen laughing, we can internally categorize our own enjoyment as "laughing with" not "laughing at."[25]

Although the segments appeared as various parts of other programs such as *The Tonight Show* and *The Garry Moore Show* during the peak popularity of *The Twilight Zone, Candid Camera* did not appear as a stand-alone program until 1960 and reached its peak popularity in 1965 as the original run of *The Twilight Zone* was ending. Indeed, in a crucial way, *Candid Camera* can be understood as the anti-*Twilight Zone*. Where *The Twilight Zone* frequently used empirical equivalence as a mechanism to generate a sense of danger in the audience, *Candid Camera* employed empirical equivalence, the same exact mechanism, as a source of playfulness. If the Jewish Serling was sending a clear message that resonated with post-Holocaust Jews that things are not always as they appear and how they really are could be extremely harmful, the Jewish Funt was saying that things not being as they appear is nothing to worry about. Why the difference?

There are two explanatory schemes that can be proposed. One is intrinsic to Jewish culture and the other is a historical-sociological account. The first proposes that humor is a coping mechanism embedded within Jewish culture. Jews are a diasporic people and the post-diaspora history of Jews, the line goes, is a tragic story of an enduring minority that suffers a seemingly endless string of attacks from the majority cultures in which its communities are embedded. Some cultures might become rebellious, lashing out at the oppression, but the Jews huddle closer and find clever

25. Nadis, "Citizen Funt," 20.

ways to make light and laugh at the situation, both with humor that mocks the oppressor and the self-effacing humor that mocks themselves for being in the situation. Sigmund Freud in his book *Jokes and Their Relation to the Unconscious* famously wrote of Jews, "I do not know whether there are many other instances of a people making fun to such a degree of its own character."[26]

In this way, one can see *Candid Camera* as being a very Jewish program. Indeed, one could even see Funt as using an endemically Jewish approach to infiltrate the broader American culture. At this point in time, heroes were portrayed as men of action, but few words. Consider Clint Eastwood's roles in the Sergio Leone spaghetti Westerns of this same period, like *Fistful of Dollars*. Eastwood is tough, silent, and unafraid to use violence to settle problems. He is the quintessential example of the Yiddish term "*goyische-kopf*," which translates literally to "non-Jewish head" and is contrasted with "*yiddische-kopf*" or "Jewish head." These are racist terms in which non-Jews are seen by Jews as collectively inferior because they lack brains and have to resort to brawn. *Goyische-kopf* designates "oaf" or "muscle-bound moron," while *yiddische-kopf* refers to cleverness, superior problem-solving ability, the ability to think oneself out of a problem.

What we see in *Candid Camera* is the private moments of those who possess a *goyische-kopf*. Many of those who are pranked are normal American (non-Jewish) men who aspire to embody the cultural understanding of masculinity, which requires being in control, calm, and stoic when things go wrong. Funt creates scenarios that directly challenge this capacity. Many men seen on the program do not laugh at the absurdity of their situation when they are in it, but often try to play it cool as if they are completely unruffled by the completely unexpected or seemingly impossible. It is not until the end that we see genuine emotion.

Candid Camera is Jews' way of finding humor in empirical equivalence because (1) we see that the world not being the way we think it is may not be dangerous, but rather can be incongruous and absurd, and (2) those who may be the threat to us are really not frightening, but very human when we see them at intimate times we ordinarily are not allowed to see. This is the first account.

The historical-sociological account contends that the reason Jews switched from seeing empirical equivalence as a source of danger and instead portrayed it as a source of playful fun is that the context of Jewish life changed from the start to the end of the run of *The Twilight Zone*. The late

---

26. Freud, *Jokes and Their Relation to the Unconscious*, 112.

1950s and early 1960s were a period of intense social change for Jews. Adolf Hitler's anti-Semitic genocide spurred many Jewish men of fighting age to join the war effort, like both Rod Serling and Allen Funt. After the war, that meant that they could partake of the benefits of the GI Bill.[27] The GI Bill both allowed Jews, who would otherwise largely not been able, to attend college and therefore gain skills and knowledge that gave them access to better jobs. It also provided government sponsored, low-interest loans that allowed Jews—who had largely been clustered in small urban areas—to purchase homes in the suburbs. Redlining did make sure these suburban homes were in exclusively Jewish neighborhoods, but they were suburban homes nonetheless.

As Jews suburbanized and found jobs in the wider economy, especially in professional fields like medicine, law, education, accounting, and science and engineering, they rapidly assimilated. This assimilation gave them "model minority" status. As the fight for civil rights for Black Americans heated up, Jews, by contrast, were seen as the good minorities, the ones who were willing to fit in, accept mainstream values, and not cause trouble. Anti-Semitism in America was far from gone, but compared to the racism directed at African Americans, it was significantly less problematic. With the racist focus of the ethnonationalists looking in a different direction, it allowed Jews a feeling of relative security. We can see ramifications of that sense of a lack of threat embodied in cultural products, including empirical equivalence-based entertainment.

As the cultural context of normal Jewish life changed, so too did the television programs they created. Both *The Twilight Zone* and *Candid Camera* utilized empirical equivalence as the central lever that propelled the programs forward, but did so in very different ways. For *The Twilight Zone* it was the basis of concern and for *Candid Camera* it was the basis of fun.

MISSION: IMPOSSIBLE AND THE EMPOWERMENT OF EMPIRICAL EQUIVALENCE

A third program, not often connected to the other two, also came to prominence for using empirical equivalence as a central recurring plot device,

---

27. It should be noted that Southern legislators made sure that the distribution of benefits under the GI Bill were under local control. This meant that structural and individual racism would make sure that the assistance would not find its way to all veterans of the war, that Black veterans would be deprived of the generational wealth that came from the aid.

Mission: Impossible. Launching in 1966, on the tail end of the heyday of the original *Candid Camera* (the show was rebooted several times in the following decades), *Mission: Impossible* was an action-adventure series focused on the Impossible Missions Force, or IMF, that resembled the Central Intelligence Agency in its use of government-sponsored covert missions.

It differed in that, unlike the CIA, the IMF was not technically part of the government and it was made clear at the beginning of each episode to its main character that "should you, or any of your IM Force, be caught or killed, the secretary will disavow any knowledge of your actions." The powers-that-be wanted them to succeed, but were in no way taking responsibility for the mission or any actions therein.

This concerned the series' creator, Bruce Geller, a Jewish writer from New York whose father had been a New York State Supreme Court justice. In his family, as in Judaism, the law is what made us humane.[28] In *Mission: Impossible*, however, the good guys were working outside of the law. As Patrick White put it:

> *Mission: Impossible* matter-of-factly offered the premise that the United States government sponsored a group of saboteurs who were answerable to no one. In the course of their duties the IMF could—and did—lie, cheat, steal, falsify media, hold persons illegally, falsely incriminate, destroy the property of innocent people, kidnap, plot (though never personally execute) assassinations, and break any civil and criminal rule that stood in their way. Individual rights were ignored.[29]

For these acts, the perpetrators were never held responsible, never faced charges, or any sort of repercussions. And, again, those were the good guys.

The actor most widely associated with the program is Peter Graves, who portrayed Jim Phelps, the head of the IMF. Graves took over that role in the second season. In the initial season, Dan Briggs was the head of the IMF, portrayed by Steven Hill, an orthodox Jew whose real name is Solomon Krakovsky. He is best remembered for his role decades later as Adam Schiff, the wise, but cranky district attorney on *Law and Order.*

Every episode begins with the head of the IMF receiving a mission in a deserted semi-public place via a recording that subsequently self-destructs. The recording never orders the mission be done, but gives the head of the IMF the option of accepting it. The offer, of course, is always accepted.

---

28. White, *The Complete* Mission: Impossible *Dossier*, 16.
29. White, *The Complete* Mission: Impossible *Dossier*, 22.

The second scene is set in the stylish '60's apartment of the IMF head who selects the crew he needs for this particular mission. While there is some variability with guest members joining the group from time to time, there are almost always four core members for any job. Two of them are not played by Jewish actors. The strong man and driver is Willy Armitage, played by Peter Lupus. Barney Collier, the wizard of technology, was played by Greg Morris. Together they tended to be the members who worked behind the scenes.

The remaining two members of the core group were played by Jewish actors. Cinnamon Carter, a fashion model turned spy, was played by Barbara Bain, whose real name was Mildred Fogel. The remaining member of the team was a magician/disguise artist. The role was initially filled by Martin Landau as Rollin Hand, who was replaced in the fifth season by Leonard Nimoy, who went by the name The Great Paris. Again, both of these actors were Jewish. At the start of the series, the majority of the IMF was comprised of Jews.

Once the team was selected, they assembled in the apartment, and discussed the plan. Questions and comments in this scene were vague and the audience was left with the sense that the team knew what they were doing, but we did not. We only knew that if every element did not go off exactly as planned, exactly when planned, things could get bad for everyone quickly.

The rest of the episode was then dedicated to the carrying out of the plan. Some of it, the viewers were in on, and some of it they were not. In nearly every case, the central concept was empirical equivalence, that is, the goal was to create an artificial reality for the mark in order to get him to do something he otherwise would not have done. The members of the IMF, through cleverness, deceit, and technology, would alter the world, making it seem to their victim different than it was in order to manipulate them.

It could be Rollin Hand, the man of a thousand faces, creating a rubber mask that makes him look identical to someone else. It could be a video projection that makes an empty jail cell seem occupied. It could be Dan Briggs having a secret code that only an insider could know. In all of these cases the IMF was making the world inhabited by their mark look one way, when it was really different. They could then exploit that misunderstanding to get the mark to confess, to change plans, or to get someone to mistakenly execute them—it was never the IMF who did the killing, but they would set people up so that others would do the job for them.

The audience granted the moral permissibility of this deception and the consequences of it on the basis of a simple utilitarian calculation. It was always made clear from the beginning of the episode that the mark was a bad person who was using violence and power in a way that would lead to horrible outcomes if allowed to proceed. The bad guys were not only horrifically bad, but also on the verge of doing something despicable. The possible end was so awful that it justified virtually any means to prevent it from occurring.

Mission: Impossible is an artifact of its time, the Cold War, and as such many of the villains are somewhere behind the Iron Curtain. The portion of the globe controlled or influenced by the Soviets included parts of Eastern and Central Europe as well as the Caribbean and South America, which meant that there were always plenty of potential targets. The countries were never actual places, but had names like "San Cordova," "Surananka," and "Svardia" that elicited an understanding of which part of the world the mission would be. Among the few episodes in which actual places and groups were referred to were three episodes in the first two seasons in which the bad guys were Nazis.

In all three of these episodes, the threat that is central to the plot is the same—a rump contingent of important former insiders of Hitler's inner circle are working to relaunch Nazism and must be stopped. In "The Legacy," aired on January 7, 1967, the sons of four of Hitler's most trusted officers gather in Buenos Aires, each with a portion of the code needed to access the Argentinian bank account that contains Hitler's fortune, which they will collectively use to reestablish Nazism in Germany. In "The Legend," aired on February 11, 1967, one of Hitler's cronies, Dr. Herbert Raynor, will be released from Spandau prison in Berlin from which he will travel to Puerto Huberra to rendezvous with another top Nazi, Martin Bormann, and according to the tape at the beginning of the episode, "Whoever is bringing them together seems to be well-financed and determined to sow the seeds of Nazism across the world again." In "Echo of Yesterday," aired on December 10, 1967, Colonel Marcus von Frank is about to take control of the largest munitions factory in Europe which he will use to arm his resurgent group of neo-Nazis. In all of these episodes, the common thread is that while World War II may have ended and the Third Reich may have been buried, the threat of Nazism reviving itself resides just below the surface and could pop up again at a moment's notice.

Rod Serling showed the same sort of thing in *The Twilight Zone* episode, "He's Alive," aired on January 24, 1963, in which a young American teenager, Peter Vollmer, played by Dennis Hopper, starts a ragtag neo-Nazi group and receives advice from a shadowy figure throughout the episode that helps him turn his failing band into a powerful neo-Nazi movement in America. The shadowy figure, of course, was Adolf Hitler and the moral to be taken away from the tragic episode is that it still could happen here in America.

But Geller's approach to the problem is quite different. In Serling's version, the question remains open whether it will happen again. Vollmer is killed in the end, but the spirit of Hitler escapes and remains loose in the world. In *Mission: Impossible*, on the other hand, the IMF team is always successful at creating a fake reality for the plotting neo-Nazis that causes them to foil their own plans.

What is crucial to this discussion is that in *Mission: Impossible*, it is the good guys who control the false, constructed reality. In *The Twilight Zone*, empirical equivalence was a source of anxiety. In *Candid Camera*, it was a source of levity. But in *Mission: Impossible*, it is a source of justice and control of a world that could be threatening. Empirical equivalence is now a tool to correct the flaws, to use the Hebrew phrase, *tikkun olam*, to heal the world.

The explanation of this shift could again reside in three simultaneous aspects of Jewish American life. The first is the continued assimilation of Jews into suburban life. This was the period where Jews started to feel more American and the Cold War created a clear dichotomy between us and them, between freedom and autocracy. As Jews began to feel a part of the American mainstream, nationalism would naturally follow.[30] *Mission: Impossible* would be an artistic expression of Jewish Americanness.

With the constant underlying threat of nuclear annihilation, Americans generally were nervous about the USSR. But the Jewish concerns about the Soviet Union were even greater. Russia was notoriously anti-Semitic, destroying synagogues, oppressing Jewish citizens, and bringing Jews to trial on trumped up charges under the age-old tropes of Jews as arch-capitalists controlling the world through financial markets.[31] Jewish refuseniks like Natan Shiransky were protesting for human rights and paying a steep price for speaking out.[32] The plight of Jews in Russian-controlled

---

30. This is, in spite of the fact that this period also contains the McCarthy Hearings and the House on Un-American Activities Committee meetings in which liberals and leftists, especially Jews, were accused of being traitorous, working with the Soviet Union. The long-standing anti-Semitic trope of Jews not being loyal to the country in which they live was leveraged to harm Jews with an interest in social justice. See Sarna, *American Judasim*, 281–85.

31. Pinkus, *The Jews of the Soviet Union*, 139–209.

32. Sharansky, *Fear No Evil*.

areas was becoming a more common topic of conversation and action by congregations.[33] Two years before the premier of *Mission: Impossible*, Jacob Birnbaum launched Student Struggle for Soviet Jewry, a group advocating for the rights of Jews in the Soviet Union.[34] Many other similar groups were created soon after. Many Jews saw the Soviet Union as the bad guys for multiple reasons.

Jewish Americans, therefore, had reasons from both sides of their hyphens to be suspicious of the Soviets and continually concerned about the revivals of the Nazis, making a show like *Mission: Impossible* appealing. The show is an action-adventure program, but what made it unique (and successful) was that unlike other more "manly" approaches to conflict, it was a show that featured success through characters using their *yiddische-kopf* in being clever to handle the danger through intellectual and creative means, and not their *goyische-kopf* in just fighting and shooting their way out.

The third cultural element is that there were real-life figures like the IMF whom Jews were actively rooting for, Nazi hunters like Simon Wiesenthal, who in 1953 found that the notorious Nazi war criminal Adolf Eichmann was hiding in Buenos Aires, Argentina. Wiesenthal notified the *Mossad*, the Israeli foreign intelligence service (information gatherers like the American NSA), who tracked Eichmann, verifying his location. In 1960, a team of *Shin Bet* agents (spies like the American CIA) sent a team of eight agents who captured him.[35] Two years later, Eichmann was tried, convicted, and executed for war crimes in Israel.[36]

There were plenty of others who had committed atrocities still out there, but in 1965 the German and Austrian governments' statute of limitations on war crimes expired, leaving former Nazi criminals free. Both governments nominally extended the date for five years, but refused to commit the resources needed to actively pursue the former members of the Third Reich's final solution.[37] This gap was filled by individuals like Wiesenthal who tracked notorious Nazis throughout the world, many in South America.

> ODESSA was believed to be an acronym for Organisation der ehemaligen SS-Angehörigen (Organization of Former SS-Members),

---

33. Sarna, *American Judaism*, 318.
34. Lazin, *The Struggle for Soviet Jewry in American Politics*, 40.
35. Segev, *Simon Wiesenthal*, 9.
36. Arendt, *Eichmann in Jerusalem*.
37. Segev, *Simon Wiesenthal*, 191.

which was seeking ways for Nazi criminals to escape and helping to smuggle them to places of refuge, mainly in South America. It was said to be an underground network with worldwide connections that worked like a well-oiled machine.[38]

The Nazis were welcomed in South America and Nazi hunters went there to find them.

This very situation, tracking Nazi war criminals in thinly veiled Latin American nations, was represented in the three episodes of *Mission: Impossible*. For Jews, the IMF was fictional, but barely so. It directly connected in their minds to covert operations actually underway by Israeli and nongovernmental agents who had to use subterfuge as one of their primary weapons.

So, when non-Jews of the time watched *Mission: Impossible*, it was yet another of a series of Cold War adventure spy thrillers that were standard fare at the time. But when Jews saw the same show, it represented something deeper.

It is worth noting one additional Jewish program of the period, which spoofed *Mission: Impossible*, James Bond, and the like: *Get Smart*. Launched and initially written by Jewish comic geniuses Mel Brooks and Buck Henry,[39] it followed the exploits of secret agent Maxwell Smart, given the comic title of "agent 86" (to 86 something is to consider it garbage and throw it away) and his partner only known by her label "agent 99." Both were played by Jewish actors, Don Adams and Barbara Feldon. Smart worked tirelessly—and often incompetently—for a thinly disguised take-off of the CIA called Control, seeking to foil the plots of the KAOS, among whose leaders was the evil German Siegfried. The name "Siegfried" is an allusion to Richard Wagner's hero in his overtly anti-Semitic Ring Cycle, a work deeply influential on Nazi mythology. The joke is not only that the Jewish agents are the good guys and the Germans the bad guys, but that Siegfried was played by Jewish actor Bernie Kopell. His sidekick was known as "Starker," which is the Yiddish term for a tough guy, although he was portrayed by non-Jew King Moody.

Control, like the IMF in *Mission: Impossible*, engages in deception to cause empirical equivalence. Smart's shoe, famously, is a telephone. Control created an automaton agent, given the Jewish name "Hymie, the robot," although played by non-Jewish comedian Dick Gautier.

---

38. Segev, *Simon Wiesenthal*, 107.
39. Parish, *It's Good to Be the King*, 165–69.

The usual victim of empirical equivalence, however, is Smart. Where the Jewish agents of the IMF employ empirical equivalence to catch the bad guys, in *Get Smart*, Smart gets them despite having fallen for the deception and then responding with the running gag that went something like, "Ah, it's the old picture in the keyhole trick. That's the second time I've fallen for it this month." So, the spoofing of *Mission: Impossible* achieves its humor through inverting the empirical equivalence that made *Mission: Impossible* the show it was.

CONCLUSION

Jews benefitted from modernism, the view that the world is a rational place and that the human mind is sufficient to understand its working. This view entailed beliefs about human equality and the universality of rights which allowed Jews to become citizens. Many Jews, like Albert Einstein, made the most of this emancipation that came from philosophy and made its way into the world. Modernity allowed them the lives of human flourishing they lived and in return they were committed to it and its scientific worldview. Seeing was believing. Believing that made their lives better.

But then came the Shoah. The persecution, the inhumanity, the hatred and dehumanization leading to genocide was the work of monsters. But they were not unknown monsters. They were people who had been friends and neighbors just a year before. They knew these had been friends. They had seen it with their own eyes . . . and seeing is believing. But now it wasn't.

In *The Twilight Zone, Candid Camera, Mission: Impossible*, and *Get Smart*, we see four instances of television series based on the same premise—that seeing is *not* believing, something that Jews had to grudgingly admit after the horrors of World War II. Aristotle, in *The Poetics*, argued for the position philosophers now call "aesthetic mimesis," the view that art imitates life.[40] We can see that in play with these four television series. Jewish art did imitate Jewish life, or at least this new lack of belief in radical empiricism. Through creative implementation of empirical equivalence, all of these series constructed unexpected twists that entertained American audiences. But the four did so in very different ways and used it to send very different messages. Those were reflections of the changes of the lives of Jews in terms of their place in American society over the course of the decade and a half from 1959 to 1973.

40. Aristotle, *Poetics*, 119.

Bibliography

Abrams, Nathan. *The New Jew in Film: Exploring Jewishness and Judaism in Cinema*. New Brunswick, NJ: Rutgers University Press, 2012.
Adams, Joey. *The Borscht Belt*. New York: Bobbs-Merrill, 1966.
Antler, Joyce. *Talking Back: Images of Jewish Women in American Popular Culture*. Hanover, NH: Brandeis University Press, 1998.
Arendt, Hannah. *Eichmann in Jerusalem: A Report on the Banality of Evil*. New York: Viking, 1963.
Aristotle. *Poetics*. Translated by Stephen Halliwell. Chicago: University of Chicago Press, 1998.
Benny, Joan. *Sunday Night at Seven: The Jack Benny Story*. New York: Warner, 1990.
Boyarin, Daniel. *Unheroic Conduct: The Rise of Heterosexuality and the Invention of the Jewish Man*. Berkeley: University of California Press, 1997.
Brodkin, Karen. *How Jews Became White Folks and What That Says about Race in America*. New Brunswick, NJ: Rutgers University Press, 1989.
Bronstein, Herbert. *A Passover Haggadah*. New York: Central Conference of American Rabbis, 1994.
Buber, Martin. *I and Thou*. Translated by Ronald Gregor Smith. New York: Scribner, 1958.
Burns, George. *Gracie: A Love Story*. New York: Penguin, 1988.
Clark, Ronald. *Einstein: The Life and Times*. New York: Hodder and Stoughton, 1972.
Dauber, Jeremy. *Jewish Comedy: A Serious History*. New York: Norton, 2013.
Dawidowicz, Lucy. "The Jewishness of the Jewish Labor Movement: in the United States." In *The American Jewish Experience*, edited by Jonathan Sarna, 185–93. New York: Holmes & Meier, 1986.
Descartes, René. *Discourse on Method for Rightly Conducting One's Reason in the Sciences*. Translated by Donald Cress. Indianapolis: Hackett, 1998.
Dillingham, William. *Dictionary of Races of Peoples*. Washington, DC: Government Printing Office, 1911.
Dorinson, Joseph. *Kvetching and Shpritzing: Jewish Humor in American Popular Culture*. Jefferson: McFarland, 2015.
Dwork, Deborah. "Immigrant Jews on the Lower East Side of New York: 1880–1914." In *The Jewish American Experience*, edited by Jonathan Sarna, 120–37. New York: Holmes and Meier, 1986.
Efron, Noah. *A Chosen Calling: Jews in Science in the Twentieth Century*. Baltimore: Johns Hopkins University Press, 2014.
Engel, Joel. *Rod Serling: The Dreams and Nightmares of Life in The Twilight Zone*. Chicago: Contemporary, 1989.

Epstein, Lawrence. *The Haunted Smile: The Story of Jewish Comedians in America.* New York: Public Affairs, 2002.

Feiner, Shmuel. *Haskalah and History: The Emergence of a Modern Jewish Historical Consciousness.* Liverpool: Liverpool University Press, 2001.

Feldman, Leslie Dale. *Spaceships and Politics: The Political Theory of Rod Serling.* Lanham, MD: Lexington, 2010.

Freud, Sigmund. *Jokes and Their Relation to the Unconscious.* Translated by James Strachey. New York: Norton. 1960.

Fried, Albert. *The Rise and Fall of the Jewish Gangster in America.* New York: Columbia University Press, 1993.

Galton, Francis. *Hereditary Genius.* London: Macmillan, 1869.

Gartner, Lloyd. "The Midpassage of American Jewry." In *The Jewish American Experience,* edited by Jonathan Sarna, 258–67. New York: Holmes and Meier, 1986.

Gay, Peter. *Freud, Jews, and Other Germans: Masters and Victims in Modernist Culture.* New York: Oxford University Press, 1979.

Gimbel, Steven. *Einstein: His Space and Times.* New Haven, CT: Yale University Press, 2015.

Gitelman, Zvi. *A Century of Ambivalence: The Jews of Russia and the Soviet Union, 1881 to the Present.* Bloomington: Indiana University Press, 1988.

Goren, Arthur. "A 'Golden Decade' for American Jews." In *The Jewish American Experience,* edited by Jonathan Sarna, 294–313. New York: Holmes and Meier, 1986.

Götz, Aly, et al. *Cleansing the Fatherland: Nazi Medicine and Racial Hygiene.* Baltimore: Johns Hopkins University Press, 1994.

Gould, Stephen Jay. *The Mismeasure of Man.* New York: Norton, 1981.

Hattam, Victoria. "Ethnicity and the Boundaries of Race: Rereading Directive 15." *Daedalus* 134.1 (2005) 61–69.

Hawkins, Mike. *Social Darwinism in European and American Thought, 1860–1945: Nature as Model and Nature as Threat.* Cambridge: Cambridge University Press, 1997.

Hegel, G. W. F. *Phenomenology of Spirit.* Translated by A. V. Miller. Oxford: Oxford University Press, 1977.

Hersch, Charles. *Jews and Jazz: Improvising Ethnicity.* New York: Taylor and Francis, 2016.

Heschel, Abraham Joshua. *Maimonides: A Biography.* Translated by Joachim Neugroschel. New York: Farrar, Strauss, Giroux, 1936.

Hobbes, Thomas. *Leviathan.* 1651. Reprint, London: J. M. Dent, 1949.

Howe, Irving. *World of Our Fathers: The Journal of the Eastern European Jews to America and the Life They Found and Made.* New York: Touchstone, 1976.

Humes, Edward. "How the GI Bill Shunted Blacks into Vocational Training." *Journal of Blacks in Higher Education* 53 (2006) 92–104.

Janus, Samuel. "The Great Comedians: Personality and Other Factors." *American Journal of Psychoanalysis* 35.2 (1975) 169–74.

Kagen, Israel Meir. *Chofetz Chaim: A Lesson a Day.* Edited by Shimon Finkleman and Yitzchak Berkowitz. Brooklyn, NY: Misorah, 1995.

Kahonen, Lina. "The Space Race and Soviet Utopian Thinking." *Sociological Review* 57.1 (2009) 114–31.

Kanfer, Stefan. *Stardust Lost: The Triumph, the Tragedy, and Mishugas of the Yiddish Theatre in America.* New York: Knopf, 2006.

BIBLIOGRAPHY

Kant, Immanuel. "Determination of the Concept of a Human Race." In *Anthropology, History, and Education*, translated by Holly Wilson, 143–62. Cambridge: Cambridge University Press, 2007.

———. *Groundwork for the Metaphysics of Morals*. Translated by Mary Gregor. Cambridge: Cambridge University Press, 1998.

Katz, Jacob. *A House Divided: Orthodoxy and Schism in Nineteenth-Century Central European Jewry*. New York: New York University Press, 1998.

Kierkegaard, Søren. *Fear and Trembling*. Cambridge: Cambridge University Press, 2006.

Klass, Judy. "*The Twilight Zone* as Jewish Science Fiction." In *Jews in Popular Science Fiction: Marginalization in the Mainstream*, edited by Valerie Estelle Frankel, 257–74. Lanham, MD: Lexington, 2022.

Kohonen, Iina. *Picturing the Cosmos: A Visual History of Early Soviet Space Endeavor*. Chicago: University of Chicago Press, 2017.

Kolodny, Ralph. "Catholics and Father Coughlin: Misremembering the Past." *Patterns of Prejudice* 19.4 (1985) 15–25.

Kraemer, Joel. *Maimonides: The Life and World of One of Civilization's Greatest Minds*. New York: Crown, 2010.

Kuenzli, Rudolf. "The Nazi Appropriation of Nietzsche." *Nietzsche-Studien Berlin* 12 (1983) 428–35.

Land, Barbara, and Myrik Land. *A Short History of Las Vegas*. Reno: University of Nevada Press, 2004.

Lazin, Fred. *The Struggle for Soviet Jewry in American Politics: Israel versus the American Jewish Establishment*. New York: Lexington, 2005.

Leibniz, Wilhelm Gottfried. "Fifth Correspondence with Clarke." In *The Leibniz-Clarke Correspondence*, translated by Henry Gavin Alexander, 55–96. New York: St. Martin's Press, 1956.

———. *Theodicy*. Translated by E. M. Huggard. LaSalle, IL: Open Court, 1990.

Levi, Primo. *The Drowned and the Saved*. New York: Simon and Schuster, 1986.

Lottman, Herbert. *The French Rothschilds: The Great Banking Dynasty through Two Turbulent Centuries*. New York: Crown, 1995.

Mandell, Richard. *The Nazi Olympics*. Urbana: University of Illinois Press, 1971.

Marcuse, Herbert. *One-Dimensional Man*. Boston: Beacon, 1964.

Merton, Robert K. "Science, Technology and Society in Seventeenth Century England." *Osiris* 4.2 (1938) 360–632.

Mettler, Suzanne. *Soldiers to Citizens: The G.I. Bill and the Making of the Greatest Generation*. New York: Oxford University Press, 2005.

Mill, John Stuart. *Utilitarianism*. London: Longman, Green, Reader, and Dyer, 1871.

Mulvey, Laura. "Visual Pleasure and Narrative Cinema." *Screen* 16.3 (1975) 6–18.

Nadis, Fred. "Citizen Funt: Surveillance as Cold War Entertainment." In *The Tube Has Spoken: Reality TV and History*, edited by Julie Anne Taddeo and Ken Dvorak, 11–26. Lexington: University Press of Kentucky, 2010.

Nesteroff, Kliph. *The Comedians: Drunks, Thieves, Scoundrels, and the History of American Comedy*. New York: Grove, 2015.

Neusner, Jacob. *Torah from Our Sages: Pirkei Avot*. Dallas: Russell, 2022.

Newton, Isaac. *Mathematical Principles of Natural Philosophy*. Berkeley: University of California Press, 1966.

Nietzsche, Friedrich. *The Gay Science*. Translated by Walter Kaufmann. New York: Vintage, 1974.

———. *On the Genealogy of Morals*. Translated by Walter Kaufmann. New York: Vintage, 1969.

Novak, William, and Moshe Waldoks. *The Big Book of Jewish Humor*. New York: HaperCollins, 1981.

Overbye, Dennis. "Gravitational Waves Detected, Confirming Einstein's Theory." *New York Times*, February 11, 2016.

Parish, James Robert. *It's Good to Be the King: The Seriously Funny Life of Mel Brooks*. New York: Wiley, 2017.

Parisi, Nicholas. *Rod Serling: His Life, Work, and Imagination*. Jackson: University of Mississippi Press, 2018.

Pelli, Moshe. *Haskalah and Beyond: The Reception of the Hebrew Enlightenment and the Emergence of Haskalah Judaism*. Lanham, MD: University Press of America, 2010.

Pinkus, Benjamin. *The Jews of the Soviet Union: The History of a National Minority*. Cambridge: Cambridge University Press, 1988.

Plato. *Crito*. Indianapolis: Hackett, 2002.

Prell, Riv-Ellen. "Why Jewish Princesses Don't Sweat: Desire and Consumption in Post-War American Jewish Culture." In *Too Jewish? Challenging Traditional Identities*, edited by Norman Keeblatt, 74–92. New York: Jewish Museum, 1998.

Proctor, Robert. *Racial Hygiene: Medicine under the Nazis*. Cambridge, MA: Harvard University Press, 1988.

Rhyder, Julia. "Festivals and Violence in 1 and 2 Maccabees: Hanukkah and Nicanor's Day." *Hebrew Bible and Ancient Israel* 10.1 (2021) 63–76.

Ribuffo, Leo. "Henry Ford and *The International Jew*." In *The Jewish American Experience*, edited by Jonathan Sarna, 201–18. New York: Holmes and Meier, 1986.

Rickles, Don. *Rickles' Book*. New York: Simon and Schuster, 2007.

Rohrbacher, Stefan. "From Württemberg to America: A Nineteenth-Century German-Jewish Village on Its Way to the New World." In *The Jewish American Experience*, edited by Jonathan Sarna, 44–59. New York: Holmes and Meier, 1986.

Rosenzweig, Franz. *The Star of Redemption*. New York: Holt, Rinehart, and Winston, 1970.

Sander, Gordon. *Serling: The Rise and Twilight of Television's Last Angry Man*. New York: Dutton, 1992.

Sarna, Jonathan. *American Judaism: A History*. New Haven, CT: Yale University Press, 2004.

Scheppler, Bill. *The Mississippi Burning Trial: A Primary Source Account*. New York: Rosen, 2003.

Scholem, Gershom. *Major Trends in Jewish Mysticism*. New York: Schocken, 1961.

Segel, Binjamin. *A Lie and a Libel: The History of the Protocols of the Elders of Zion*. Translated by Richard Levy. Lincoln: University of Nebraska Press, 1926.

Segev, Tom. *Simon Wiesenthal: The Life and Legends*. New York: Knopf, 2012.

Serling, Anne. *As I Knew Him: My Father, Rod Serling*. New York: Citadel, 2013.

Sharansky, Natan. *Fear No Evil*. New York: Public Affairs, 1998.

Simon, Ron. "The Changing Definition of Reality Television." In *Thinking Outside the Box: A Contemporary Television Genre Reader*, edited by Brian Geoffrey Rose and Gary Edgerton, 179–200. Lexington: University of Kentucky Press, 2005.

Singer, Merrill, and Greg Mirhej. "High Notes: The Role of Drugs in the Making of Jazz." *Journal of Ethnicity in Substance Abuse* 5.4 (2006) 1–36.

Spencer, Herbert. *Social Statics; or, The Conditions Essential to Human Happiness Specified, and the First of Them Developed*. London: John Chapman, 1851.

Spencer, Hugh. "Social Justice from the *Twilight Zone*: Rod Serling as Human Rights Activist." *Dialogue: The Interdisciplinary Journal of Popular Culture and Pedagogy* 5.1 (2018). http://journaldialogue.org/issues/v5-issue-1/social-justice-from-the-twilight-zone-rod-serling-as-human-rights-activist/.

Steinsaltz, Adin. *The Essential Talmud*. New York: Basic, 1976.

Steinschneider, Mortiz. "An Introduction to the Arabic Literature of the Jews." *Jewish Quarterly* 13 (1905) 92–110.

Stern, Stephen. *The Unbinding of Isaac: A Phenomenological Midrash of Genesis 22*. Bern: Lang, 2012.

Stratton, Jon. "Not Really White—Again: Performing Jewish Difference in Hollywood Films since the 1980s." *Screen* 42.2 (2001) 142–66.

Supple, Barry. "A Business Elite: German-Jewish Financiers in Nineteenth Century New York." In *The Jewish American Experience*, edited by Jonathan Sarna, 99–112. New York: Holmes and Meier, 1986.

Sweet, Jeffrey. *Something Wonderful Right Away: An Oral History of Second City and the Compass Players*. New York: Limelight, 1987.

Telushkin, Joseph. *Jewish Humor: What the Best Jewish Jokes Say about the Jews*. New York: Morrow, 1998.

Thayer, Ernest. "Casey at the Bat: A Ballad of the Republic, Sung in the Year 1888." *Daily Examiner*, June 3, 1888.

Warren, Donald. *Radio Priest: Charles Coughlin, the Father of Hate Radio*. Ann Arbor: University of Michigan Press, 1996.

Weiss, Bari. *How to Fight Antisemitism*. New York: Crown, 2021.

White, Patrick. *The Complete* Mission: Impossible *Dossier*. New York: Avon, 1981.

Wiggin, Kate Douglas, and Nora Archibald Smith. *The Arabian Nights*. New York: Scribner, 1909.

Wisse, Ruth. *No Joke: Making Jewish Humor*. Princeton: Princeton University Press, 2013.

Young, Patrick. "When a Day Remembers: A Performative History of Yom Ha-Shoah." *History and Memory* 2.2 (1990) 54–75.

Youngman, Henny. *Take My Wife, Please! Henny Youngman's Giant Book of Jokes*. Secaucus, NJ: Carol, 1998.

Zeitchik, Chaim Ephraim. *Sparks of Mussar: A Treasury of the Words and Deeds of the Mussar Greats*. Spring Valley, NY: Feldheim, 1985.

Zeitlin, Solomon. "Hanukkah: Its Origin and Its Significance." *Jewish Quarterly Review* 29.1 (1938) 1–36.

Index

Adams, Don, 121
Adler, Luther, 31
Akins, Claude, 86
Aleichem, Sholem, 9
Alexander II, 10
Allen, Woody, 71
antisemitism, 2–5, 10, 12, 29, 32–36, 38–40, 45, 50–67, 68, 70, 103, 106, 115, 119, 121
Aristotle 101, 122

Bain, Barbara, 117
Basehart, Richard, 94
Benny, Jack, 69, 71
Beregi, Oscar, 33
Bernstein, Abe, 60
Berg, Dick, 24
Berg, Gertrude, 59
Bergman, Ingmar, 54
Berle, Milton, 71
Berman, Shelley, 75–76
Birns, Shondor, 60
Bishop, Joey, 61
Bloomingdale, Joseph, 55
Bloomingdale, Lyman, 55
Bochner, Lloyd, 91
Bower, Antoinette, 95
Bradbury, Ray, 21
Brenner, David, 75
Brice, Fanny, 52, 78
Bridges, Lloyd, 22
Buber, Martin, 46–48
Burke, Walter, 66
Burnett, Carol 77
Burns, George, 68, 71
Brooks, Mel, 121

Caesar, Sid, 71
Candid Camera, 98, 107, 110–15
Chaney, James, 39
Cold War, 1, 6, 7, 25, 39, 108, 110, 118–19, 121
Comi, Paul, 82
Constantine, Michael, 65
Cooper, Meyer, 10–11
Copernicus, Nicholaus, 101, 109
Coughlin, Charles, 51, 56, 67, 70

Darwin, Charles, 3, 109
Dauber, Jeremy, 68
David, Larry, 71
Davis, Sammy, 61
de Leon, Moses, 100–101
Descartes, René, 101
Devine, Andy, 85
de Witt, Jacqueline, 58
Dixon, Ivan, 65, 66
Donath, Ludwig, 36
Dorinson, Joseph, 68
Dorsey, Tommy, 64

Eastwood, Clint, 114
Eichmann, Adolf, 120
Einstein, Albert, 104–5
Engel, Joel, 12
Epstein, Lawrence, 52
Euchel, Isaac Abraham, 103
eugenics, 3, 49

Feldon, Barbara, 121
Finkl, Fyvush, 69
Ford, Henry, 2, 51, 56, 67, 70
Franciscus, James, 30

INDEX

Freud, Sigmund, 114
Funt, Allen, 110–15

Galton, Francis, 3
Gautier, Dick, 121
Geller, Bruce, 116
Get Smart, 121, 122
Getz, Stan, 64
G.I. Bill, 2, 4, 15, 34
Gimbel, Adam, 55
Godfrey, Arthur, 111
Goethals, George Washington, 11
Goldberg, Rube, 69
Goldman, Marcus, 55
Goodman, Andrew, 39
Goodman, Benny, 64
Gould, Harold, 94
Graves, Peter, 116
Grinnage, Jack, 74
Gross, Milt, 69

halakhic law, 27, 35, 47
Haskalah, 38, 101
Haugen, Oren, 13
Heflin, Van, 19
Hegel, Friedrich, 45
Henry, Buck, 121
Hill, Steven, 116
Hitler, Adolf, 2, 13, 15, 32, 33, 38, 40, 42–43, 49, 56, 90, 92, 104, 110, 115, 118–119
Hobbes, Thomas, 47
Holliday, Billie, 64,
Holocaust, 2, 20, 21, 24, 28, 35, 36, 38, 67, 69, 70, 113
Holliman, Earl, 1, 107
Hoover, Herbert, 15
Hopper, Dennis, 36, 118
Horne, Geoffrey, 89
Horton, Russell, 59
Horvath, Charles, 66
Howe, Irving, 70

Janiss, Vivi, 31
Janus, Samuel, 68
Jim Crow, 4, 8, 25

Kant, Immanuel, 46

Kiel, Richard, 91
Kelly, Grace, 73
Kierkegaard, Søren, 62
Klein, Robert, 75
Klugman, Jack, 59, 63
Kopell, Bernie, 121
Kristallnacht, 51, 71
Ku Klux Klan, 39, 65

Landau, Martin, 117
Lane, Rusty, 42
Lansky, Meyer, 60
Launer, Saul John, 60
Lehman, Henry, 55
Lehrer, Tom, 71
Leibniz, Gottfried, 101, 107
Leone, Sergio, 114
Levi, Primo, 95, 109
Levy, Melvin, 14
Lewis, Richard, 71
Lindbergh, Charles, 2
Lindsey, George, 65
Livingstone, Mary, 71
Lorre, Peter, 73
Lovecraft, H.P., 21
Lupus, Peter, 117

Maimonides, 100, 104, 110
Mandell, Richard, 42, 43
Marcuse, Herbert, 70
Maross, Joe, 86
Martin, Dean, 61
Martin, Kreg, 60
Marx Brothers, 52, 70, 78, 79
May, Elaine, 75
Mazursky, Paul, 89
McCarthyism, 29, 97
McDowall, Roddy, 82
Mendelsohn, Moses, 103
Meredith, Burgess, 56, 73
Mill, John Stuart, 46
Mission: Impossible, 7, 98, 107, 115–22
Mogulesko, Sigmund, 68
Moody, King, 121
Morris, Greg, 117
Mulvey, Laura, 47
Mystery Science Theatre 3000, 80

INDEX

Nazism, 2, 3, 6, 13, 19–20, 26–39, 40, 42–43, 49–50, 63, 67, 68, 81, 83–84, 92, 97, 109, 118–19, 120–21
Newton, Isaac, 30, 101, 103
Nichols, Mike, 75
Nietzsche, Friedrich, 30, 43–46, 57
Nimoy, Leonard, 117
Novak, William, 68
nuclear weapons, 2, 6, 119

Osmond, Cliff, 89

Parker, Charlie, 64
Persoff, Nehemiah, 29
Pincon, Molly, 69
Planck, Max, 105
Posten, Tom, 73
Protocols of the Elders of Zion, 56

racism, 4–6, 18, 19, 21, 22, 25, 28, 40, 57, 63, 66, 67, 114, 115
Rankin, John, 4
Reles, Abe, 60
Rich, Buddy, 64
Rickles, Don, 73–74
Riefenstahl, Leni, 42–43
Ritz Brothers, 70
Rivers, Joan, 75
Robards, Jason, 73
Rooney, Mickey, 20
Roosevelt, Franklin Delano, 15
Rosenzweig, Franz, 80, 84
Ruskin, Joseph, 31

Sachs, Samuel, 55
Sahl, Mort, 71
Schultz, Dutch, 60
Schwerner, Mickey, 39
Seigel, Benjamin, 60
Seinfeld, Jerry, 76
Serling, Anne, 10, 16, 17, 25
Serling, Carolyn, 16–17
Serling, Esther, 10
Serling, Isaac, 10
Serling, Robert, 12
Serling, Rod
    awards, 14, 20
    career, 17–25
    childhood, 11–12
    college years, 15–17
    military service, 13–14
    radio career, 16
    television writer, 17–25
    secular Judaism, 5, 6, 7, 8, 17, 25, 38, 40, 50, 63, 69
Serling, Samuel, 10, 11
Shatner, William, 106
Shaw, Artie, 64
Sherman, Chink, 60
Sills, Paul, 75
Silvers, Phil, 71
Sinatra, Frank, 73–74
Skolnick, Menasha, 69
Sloane, Everett, 19
Sofaer, Abraham, 41
Sofer, Moishe, 103
Soros, George, 32
Sorrells, Robert, 41
Spencer, Herbert, 3, 9
Spolin, Viola, 75
Stalin, Josef, 90

Talmud, 7, 15, 26, 27, 35, 56, 80–97
Telushkin, Joseph, 68
Thayer, Ernest Lawrence, 40–41
Three Stooges, 52, 70, 78
Till, Emmitt, 63
Tucker, Sophie, 52, 78
Twilight Zone episodes
    "The Big Tall Wish," 66
    "Cavender Is Coming," 76–79
    "Death's Head Revisited," 33–36
    "The Gift," 89–91
    "The Happy Place," 21
    "He's Alive," 36–39
    "Hocus Pocus and Frisbee," 85–86
    "I Am the Night—Color Me Black," 65–66
    "In Praise of Pip," 59–63
    "Judgement Night," 29–31
    "The Little People," 86–88
    "The Man in the Bottle," 31–33
    "The Mighty Casey," 40–49
    "The Mind and the Matter," 74–76
    "Mr. Dingle, the Strong," 70–74
    "Nightmare at 20,000 Feet," 106

INDEX

(Twilight Zone *episodes, continued*)
    "One for the Angels," 52–55
    "A Passage for Trumpet," 63–64
    "People Are Alike All Over," 82–84
    "Probe 7—Over and Out," 94–97
    "The Time Element," 21
    "Time Enough at Last," 55–59
    "To Serve Man," 91–93
    "Where Is Everybody?," 1, 107–9

Vargas, Edmund, 89

Wagner, Richard, 57, 121
Warden, Jack, 41

White, Jesse, 76
White, Patrick, 116
Wiesel, Elie, 9
Wiesenthal, Simon, 120–21
Wilson, Michael, 23
Wisse, Ruth, 68
World War I, 105
World War II, 4, 6, 8, 13, 15, 18, 25, 29, 32, 34, 36, 38, 50, 68, 73, 98, 107, 110, 118, 122,
Wynn, Ed, 20, 52

Youngman, Henny, 71

www.ingramcontent.com/pod-product-compliance
Lightning Source LLC
Chambersburg PA
CBHW031324160426
43196CB00007B/661